University of London
Institute of United States Studies Monographs

2

A Tug of Loyalties
Anglo-American Relations 1765–85

Institute of United States Studies Monographs

A TUG OF LOYALTIES

Anglo-American Relations 1765-85

edited by

ESMOND WRIGHT

UNIVERSITY OF LONDON
Published for the
Institute of United States Studies
THE ATHLONE PRESS 1975

Published by
THE ATHLONE PRESS
UNIVERSITY OF LONDON
at 4 Gower Street, London WC1

Distributed by Tiptree Book Services Ltd
Tiptree, Essex

U.S.A. and Canada
Humanities Press Inc, New York

0 485 12902 7

Printed in Great Britain by
WESTERN PRINTING SERVICES LTD
BRISTOL

Preface

The papers printed here represent the lectures delivered in 1972 at a colloquium held at the Institute of United States Studies in the University of London. These colloquia, assisted by a grant from the United States Information Service, have been an annual feature of the work of the Institute since its inception. Since 1971 their proceedings have appeared in print; this volume's predecessor was *The American Environment*, edited by Professor W. R. Mead.

As the bicentenaries of the Declaration of Independence and of the beginnings of the War of Independence approach, it is proper for a British Institute to note the role played—or not played—in the years of the Revolutionary War by those now called Loyalists. They were at the time better known as the American Sufferers, since they lost heavily by the coming of the war, and inundated successive British Governments with claims for and evidence of their losses. As a consequence, rarely has an event in history been so abundantly chronicled (in the Audit Office Papers in the Public Record Office) as the circumstances of their plight, and rarely has it been so easy to mark the remorseless transition from 'loyalty' to 'treason'. It becomes indeed clear that the conflict was not between loyalist and traitor but between two forms of loyalty.

The significance of the Loyalists, however, goes beyond the events of their own time. It is important that history should be told not only 'from the bottom up', as the New Left historians like to put it, but from the vantage point of the defeated, as well as from the standpoint of the victors. Equally it is important to recall that British policies in the late eighteenth century were for the most part remarkably liberal—and indeed, except in the mainland colonies south of Massachusetts, remarkably successful. The Loyalists, although losers in one America, were the

Founding Fathers of Canada, and Canadian nationalism is their residuary legacy; with them, in a new and distinct sense, Canadian history begins. Only in the mainland colonies of North America did things go wrong. But the divide here was total—not just between Mother Country and Colony, but inside families, dividing father from son, and brother from brother, for it turned on what was meant by 'rights' and 'justice', and to whom or what one was loyal.

For the real significance of any study of the Loyalists lies in the evidence they give of their response to the crisis of their times. Loyalty has been tested in almost every generation of American history since their day, and notably in the generations from Sumter to Saigon. The late G. N. D. Evans printed some extracts on this theme in his *Allegiance in America, The Case of the Loyalists* (Reading, Mass., 1969). In the course of it he said:

What men do in unpredicted situations, the choices they make based on considerations of personal ethics, inculcated traditions, fear of authority, self-interest, and patterns of group response, remain questions to which we have only incomplete answers.

Perhaps these four papers offer some answers, however incomplete, to these recurring questions.

Contents

The Loyalists in Britain

ESMOND WRIGHT

The United States and, even more curiously, British historians of America have been slow to comprehend the nature of, and slower still to study, American Loyalism. It is in the truest sense the still all-but-totally-neglected and all-but-totally unre-searched aspect of the Revolution. Despite the fact that this was the first American Civil War, despite the fact that there was considerable contemporary published loyalist writing—by e.g. Thomas Hutchinson, Jonathan Boucher, Joseph Galloway, George Chalmers, and Daniel Leonard—and despite some contemporary historians like David Ramsay, Charles Stedman, and Alexander Graydon, who were very fair in their treatment of the Loyalists, they have commanded strikingly less interest in Britain than did the South and its cause 80 years later. And one can but begin by asking the question why didn't 1776 stir the imagination of American and British poets and historians, in the same measure as the stories and legends of the blue and the gray? If loyalty to his state made Robert E. Lee an honour-able man why does the same aura not attach itself to Thomas Hutchinson? If Lincoln was right to suppress an armed rebel-lion by force, why was not it also right for George III? If Nathan Hale has statues to him as hero, why hasn't Moses Dunbar? If Marion the swamp-fox was a hero, why was Butler the Ranger a villain? But the questions that arise are not only questions of personal loyalty, or of the harrowing facts of families divided: like the Randolphs, the Fairfaxes, the Ruggles, the Dulanys, the Coffins, the Bulls of South Carolina, the Franklins, or the Curwens—although the readiness of Samuel Curwen to go into exile may have been in part due to his knowledge of his wife's fear of the sea, for he may well have found her more troublesome than any mob. But alongside the families divided there were also profound social consequences.[1]

A conservative element of some 80–100 000 people was removed from a still new and fast-growing society—and Jeffersonian aristocracy rapidly became Jacksonian democracy. Had there been no Loyalist emigration, there might have been from the start in the New World the more familiar problems of class and social division that marked the Old. The act of banishment passed in Massachusetts, September 1778, lists 310 names. It reads, says M. C. Tyler, like 'a beadroll of the oldest and noblest families concerned in the founding and upbuilding of New England civilisation'. More than 60, he says with pride, were Harvard graduates. R. R. Palmer believes that given the difference in the populations, the exile of the Loyalists was more significant in the American story (24 emigrés per 1000 of the population) than was the migration of the emigrés from France in and after 1789 (5 emigrés per 1000). This has had the curious consequence that the parties of high conservatism in the United States, few and fugitive though they are, have found other and exotic gods to worship. Nineteenth-century capitalists found in Alexander Hamilton their advocate and made of him the apostle of big business and the gospel of wealth, although to John Adams he was 'the Creole adventurer', 'the Creole bastard'. More recent American Conservatives have looked for their prototypes not to Hutchinson and Galloway but to John Adams, revolutionary turned crusty, to John Randolph, Virginian eccentric turned crank, or to John Calhoun, the voice of a beleaguered minority. The Conservatism that has been cultivated in recent years in the United States has been post-revolutionary, a defence of the *status quo post bellum*. Americans cherish the myth that they were born free, that they inherited Liberalism without having to fight for it. In fact their story begins in rebellion, civil war and disloyalty. If it succeeds, none can call it treason.[2]

One reason for the neglect of the Loyalists in Britain is presumably that they are seen as a politically sensitive subject. Certainly they have been almost as unlucky in their history as in their lives. Perhaps it is not insignificant to recall the fate that befell the papers of Daniel Parker Coke, one of the first Claims Commissioners. They were edited by Professor H. E. Egerton, in the volume entitled 'The Royal Commission on the

Losses and Services of the American Loyalists', and published as a memorial to Whitelaw Reid, the American Ambassador in the first World War. Surplus copies of them were shipped to the United States in 1915, designed presumably as British ammunition in the battle for the American mind in the first World War. Published in a very handsome format by the Roxburghe Club, they were sent over on the good ship *Arabic*, which was, unfortunately, torpedoed by a German submarine; so they lie unread, at the bottom of the sea. Germans could smile, it seemed, and so could all Patriots. In 1915 as in 1776 God was firmly on the side of the Whigs.[3]

But it is not difficult to see why British historians have neglected the Loyalists, as they were neglected by contemporaries. Whig historiography has been as dominant in Britain as it has been in the United States. For two centuries the Whig dogs had the best of it, and impartiality about the American Revolution was in Britain an un-British, as in America it has been an un-American activity. Professor Namier worked the beginnings of a change, and thanks largely to Professor Butterfield we have recently rediscovered Adolphus. But British historical writing, like British politics, has always been pragmatic. Whether the event is 1649, 1660, 1688 or 1776, British historians have always followed the pragmatist path, addicts of what is successful in large measure just because it is so. John Adams was received at George III's court within three years of the ending of the war; one of the most delightful pieces of eighteenth-century correspondence are the warm exchanges between George Washington and Sir John Sinclair, the Caithness agricultural reformer. Moreover, the immediate impact of the Revolution and of the British failure was a total revulsion from colonies; it was another sixty years before the erratic Lord Durham produced his federal plans for Canada, and we are today learning all too sharply that they have not proved to be the final solution for Canada, or for anywhere else.

The Raj came only in the late nineteenth century and lasted a very short time. Perhaps it is easier these days to accept the fact of British defeat and of the strategic and political factors that cause it; and perhaps the very experience of failure is deemed nowadays worth a study. Certainly one of the most significant and eloquent pieces of writing on the Civil War is Vann Woodward's essay 'The Burden of Southern History', in which he reminds us that the South is the only area in the United States that experienced civil war, defeat and military occupation, and that after the harrowing it 'remains obstinately there'. If Dixie is the American historians' Vietnam, perhaps we should see the Loyalists as ours. At least the Loyalists serve, alike for American and British, as a corrective to the success ethic of the Yankees. When Elisha Hutchinson, second son of the Governor, went from Birmingham to London on a visit to his dying father, he wrote to his wife, 2 April 1780, 'A change-able planet must have ruled when I was born, for I have been tossing and tossed about in a troubled ocean from that time to the present.' History is as much a story of defeat as of victory and fair play demands study of all sides of a question. Despite Chesterton, not all historians are perpetual snobs.[4]

There is a further reason why study of the Loyalists has been difficult. Whatever their status in the New World, the leading Loyalists were of a secondary social rank in the Old, and, it seems, were quickly geographically scattered. Nor are we as yet very clear where and how they lived. Governor Hutchinson lived in some state in London, was entertained by Lord Dart-mouth, and was offered and refused a title; he died in Brompton Row, 3 June 1780. In 1776 he was providing food and shelter for 25 Loyalist refugees; his neighbours included Jonathan Sewall, John Randolph and Samuel Curwen. In the Claims Commission evidence, however, there are over 5000 Loyalist names and only Hutchinson, Galloway, Curwen, Sewall, Knox and Cruger are familiar among them.[5]

The core of the Loyalist London colony were of course those who left Boston with Howe in 1776 and came to London *via* Halifax. We know that 1100 sailed away from Boston in March 1776. Of these, 102 were members of council, customs officers and officials; 18 were clergy; 213 were Boston merchants or similar people; 382 were farmers and traders; 705 came not from Boston itself but from towns or villages nearby. They did not all sail on to Britain but it seems that at least 70 families did. Where and how did they all live, and on what? Why had they such a small influence on policy? What was the size and significance of their colonies in Bristol, Bath, Birmingham and else-where? We have some answers to these questions from Mary Beth Norton's study of the Loyalist exiles, *The British Americans*, even if this is a study confined to those of them in London, and from the new edition of Samuel Curwen's *Journal*. There is certainly here rich material, not only for the historian but for the historical sociologist. But a glance at the very valuable sources listed in the Crick and Alman *Guide* reveals how widely scattered are the Loyalist Papers—Sheffield, Stafford, Oxford, Bristol and Whitehaven, to mention but a few; and this is re-inforced by comparing them with the sources cited in the fifteenth volume of Lawrence Gipson's monumental work on *The British Empire before the American Revolution*.[6]

It is not, of course, true to say that there has been a total neglect of the Loyalists. The first American historian to give the Loyalists their due was that gifted amateur Lorenzo Sabine who published in 1847 his biographical sketches which he amplified seventeen years later. It is a work to which there is still no rival, the first piece of oral history ever attempted and done with dedication. It could well be argued that one of the real needs in the field is a new Sabine, a new biographical dictionary of the Loyalists along Namier-like lines. Moses C. Tyler published in 1897 his *Literary History of the American Revolution*, and also a famous article in the first number of the *A.H.R.* in 1895 on the Loyalists. This reflected the interest of his period in Anglo-American relations, and had indeed something of a WASP character. In his eyes 'The Tories of the Revolution' had among them 'a very considerable portion of the most refined, thought-ful and conscientious people in the colonies.' But it was an attempt to portray what he called the inward history of the revolution, the history of its ideas, motives and passions; he had the great merit of shifting the emphasis from the purely political story to intellectual relations, and he brought remarkable qualities of objectivity and grace to that task. But it is still true to say that there is only one coherent study of the political role of the Loyalists other than William Nelson's essay, and that is Claude Van Tyne's book of 1902. His scholarship is open to some criticism, and he has no bibliography; and he appears to have made very little use of the transcripts of Loyalist claims which Benjamin Stevens had already listed from his work in the P.R.O. in the 1880s. But his book was the first clear study of the Loyalists, and it is perhaps a tribute to his objectivity that his text book for schools had the merit of being banned in the schools of Battle Creek, Michigan, because in his writing and for the first time there was a departure from the straight re-telling of the patriot story.[7]

In the half century that followed Van Tyne's book there were a few studies of the Loyalists, state by state: James Stark's study of the Loyalists in Massachusetts, published in 1910; Otis Hammond's *The New Hampshire Loyalists* in 1917; Edward Jones's study of the Loyalists in New Jersey in 1927; and Isaac Harrell's study of the Virginia Loyalists published in 1926. But perhaps in this period the most significant contributions were the biography of Jared Ingersoll by Lawrence Gipson in 1920, and the series of articles by Wilbur Siebert of Ohio State University. In the same period a number of sources became available. In 1905 the Archives of Ontario published the notes of some of the commissioners on the claims of the Loyalists. A decade later the notes of D. P. Coke, another of the commissioners, were edited and published in London. Then in the 1920s and the 1930s Edward Jones published his study of Massachusetts Loyalists, and a number of Loyalist diaries and journals appeared. Especially useful were Jonathan Boucher's *Reminiscences* (1925), Alexander Chesney's *Journal* (1921), Ann Hulton's *Letters* (1927) and Samuel Seabury's *Letters* (1930).[8]

In the last few years there has been an even more dramatic change. Arthur Schlesinger Sr, *Prelude to Independence, the Newspaper War on Britain* published in 1957 pays as much attention to the Loyalist editors as to the Patriot; and John Bakeless's *Turncoats, Traitors and Heroes*, published in 1959, discusses spying and counterfeiting on both sides of the line. In 1961 there appeared a scholarly edition of Peter Oliver's *Origin and Progress*, and William Nelson's essay *The American Tory*. Since then we have had L. S. F. Upton's edition of Chief Justice William Smith's Diary (1963/65) and his biography of Smith (*The Loyal Whig*, 1969), Callahan's two volumes (1963/67), Wallace Brown's two studies, *The King's Friends* (1964) and *The Good Americans* (1965), and William Benton's interesting intellectual history, *Whig Loyalism* (1969). And a major continuing Loyalist source-book is Clifford K. Shipton's *Biographical Sketches of those who attended Harvard College.*[9]

To these titles it should be added that there have been from Paul Smith in his *Loyalists and Redcoats* (1964) and from Piers Mackesy in *The War in America* (1964), for the first time two assessments of the impact of the Loyalists on the actual campaigns. This is perhaps the most intractable subject of all, and perhaps neither of them can be described as a definitive study. What remains missing on this head is the evidence of the part actually played by the Loyalists in particular military situations. In Dr Smith's study for instance a number of regiments are mentioned—Allan MacLean's, Francis Legge's and Joseph Gorham's Fencibles; for the most part however Dr Smith gives us a survey of the war proving the familiar point that the Loyalists were inadequately used, when what one wants are details of what they did or failed to do state by state and battle by battle. There appear to be at least 62 Loyalist regiments cited in the P.R.O. papers although some of these may well be duplicates of the same regiment. Paul Smith lists 41 and concludes that 19 000 Loyalists were in the Provincial Line. Alongside the well known names, the Loyal Americans, Colonel Butler's Rangers, the Royal Greens, The Orange Rangers and the King's Royal Regiment, are those more exotic titles, the Roman Catholic Volunteers, the Royal American Reformers, the Black Pioneers and not least the Ethiopian Regiment. If there were 10 000 in the provincial line by 1780, one needs a precise account of who and where they were, how they were recruited and organized, and what they did.[10]

In our research into Loyalist material in British archives, we are ignoring both the Canadian story, on which a team of people in Fredericton, New Brunswick are engaged—it is unnecessary to emphasize the role played in Canadian History by the United Empire Loyalists—and again we are ignoring the American side of the story, and the involved problems of Article 5 of the Treaty of Peace. Thus far we have worked through the Audit Office Papers on the Loyalist claims and the vast amount of material on the Loyalists in the C.O.5 archive, (1400 volumes). We are for the time being ignoring the material in the War Office papers, though a passing tribute should be paid to the value and the quality of George Reese's volume on the Cornwallis papers that derived from the Virginia Colonial Project. A quick glance at Crick and Alman's *Guide* shows that there are at least a dozen cities which have material on the Loyalists, and this is an area we are now examining.

It still remains true, however, that in Britain any serious study of the Loyalists, in particular of their role in Britain in the War and in the peace, must start with the evidence put before the parliamentary Select Committee set up to examine their claims and the evidence submitted to it. Some 5000 Loyalists submitted claims for losses. The Government had been paying some of them quarterly allowances for some years but on no clear formula. The usual rate was at £100 a year—just adequate for a single man if he lived in a 'genteel but economic stile', as was said of Philip Key of Maryland. Since 1779 there had been in existence a Loyalist Association, the President of which was Sir William Pepperell, grandson of the conqueror of Louisburg. Since he had lost his estates in Maine, the Government were paying him a pension of £500 a year, and his house in Portman Square, along with Governor Hutchinson's home, became a Loyalist H.Q. Here met the Board of Agents who handled the Loyalist claims.

The Loyalist claims became of course a major matter of dissension in the peace negotiations, since Britain could not abandon subjects whose only crime had been their loyalty to the Crown. Shelburne admitted, however, that the claims of the Loyalists were very confused and 'required to be investigated before their claims could be enforced'. The question of Loyalist property, stubbornly argued by both sides, became the principal obstacle to delay in the final peace settlement. In the end the British government wisely gave way, on the ground that the cost of continuing the war for no purpose would be far greater than any claims they might be called upon to meet. On their side, the Americans agreed that there should be no further seizure of estates or persecution of Loyalists, and that persons having rights in any confiscated property should be allowed to seek by all lawful means to regain them. They also agreed that Congress should recommend to the State Legislatures an amnesty and the restitution of property. But by the same token the inclusion of these clauses in the Treaty of Peace made it inopportune for the British Government hastily to compensate the Loyalists.

Meanwhile in 1782 Shelburne appointed two M.P.s—John Eardley-Wilmot and Daniel Parker Coke—to enquire into the cases of what were first called the 'American Sufferers', those already in exile in Britain and in need. His point was the simple and familiar one that the government was spending too much money (although the amount had already been reduced from £80 000 to £43 000 a year), and that the sum given to the Loyalists must reach a limit. A judgment had to be formed on these claims, he said, by some impartial person or persons. And when Coke accepted Wilmot's invitation to join him, in a letter dated 25 September 1782, he did so because he recognized 'the necessity there is at this moment for the strictest economy in every department of state'. They were independent M.P.s, and both of them had been in opposition to the government's American policy. Wilmot was the son of a judge and himself a Master of Chancery. He represented Tiverton from 1776 to 1784, and Coventry from 1784 to 1796. He had sought to give the Americans some satisfaction on the issue of taxation, and in his own words 'to revise the laws by which they might think themselves aggrieved'. In an anonymous pamphlet of 1778, *A Short Defence of the Opposition*, he criticized the use of force against them. Here he differed from many Loyalists, torn between the wish to end the separation by force and violence and reluctant pride in American success. From 1784 onwards he supported Pitt. Coke was Member of Parliament for Derby from 1776 to 1780 and thereafter until 1812 for Nottingham, and though a Tory he took an independent and at times erratic line —he was a keen advocate of taxing the clergy, who were, he said, 'the most useless order of ecclesiastics'—and he seemed to see in a 40s. tax on gravestones and a tax on dogs untapped sources of largesse. His political skill is not, despite this, to be under-rated. At the general election of 1784 he declared in his election address in Nottingham that he declined 'entering into the discussion of political questions as they very often caused confusion'. He would 'vote and act as he was conscious he had theretofore done, without any view of place or emoluments, but from principle and a thorough conviction of the side he should take being right'. Needless to say, holding such impeccable principles, he was returned unopposed. Those were the days. He too was a critic of the war. But on the entry of France he had called for 'the most spirited exertions', for America was now, he said, 'the confederate of the House of Bourbon'.

But the two of them took the job on, expecting it could be done in two or three months; in fact it took the next seven years. They were more fortunate and better equipped than some later Select Committees. They were provided with a house, Newcastle house, in Lincoln's Inn Fields, and two secretaries, John Foster and Charles Monro. They insisted on being unpaid; they insisted on the physical presence of all applicants; they insisted on interviews in secrecy and on a serious judicial probing enquiry, with written submissions in advance or supporting evidence. They found that the Treasury was paying out money to 315 people; 56 of these did not appear when summoned and another 25 did not press their claim, but before they could pronounce upon the remainder, 428 new cases were added, for by 1782–3 many more refugees were arriving. The two M.P.s drew up a series of measuring rods, of which need, losses and active military service were their guides. They refused to consider losses for lands bought or improved during the war; for uncultivated lands; for property mortgaged to its full value or with defective titles; for ships captured by Americans or damage done by British troops, or for forage used by or furnished to them. Losses due to a fall in the value of provincial paper money, to robbery, or runaway negroes, or to trading setbacks, to crops left on the ground or evaded rents, were similarly disregarded. Nothing was allowed for expenses or suffering in prison, fines paid for refusing to drill with the patriot militia, or the cost of living in New York city during the war. Anticipated professional profits and losses in trade and labour were thrown out. Claims were allowed only for losses of property through loyalty, for loss of offices held before the war, and for the loss of actual professional income. But by July 1784, against claims totalling over seven million pounds, they had been able to investigate only cases involving just over half a million pounds.

In 1783 an Act was passed to go beyond the temporary provisions of Wilmot and Coke, and to appoint Commissioners, of whom they were to be two, 'to enquire into the circumstances and former fortunes of such persons as are reduced to distress by the late unhappy dissensions in America'. Of the three additional Commissioners, two had their own claims to a footnote in history. Colonel Robert Kingston had been Burgoyne's Adjutant General and had negotiated the surrender of 1777. Colonel Thomas Dundas had carried Cornwallis' surrender to Washington at Yorktown in 1781.

This Act expired in 1785, but was then renewed when the Government asked Parliament to distribute the sum of £150 000 in part payment of claims already decided on. The commission sat at first in England, but soon realized that, to give fair opportunities to all classes of claimants, it would be necessary to go to them. Thereupon, Dundas and Jeremy Pemberton, who had replaced Coke in 1785, went to Nova Scotia, and John Anstey to New York. Between the years 1785–9, these commissioners sat in Halifax, St John's, Quebec and Montreal, and Anstey stayed two years in New York. When in June 1785 the point was made in Parliament that more publicity should be given to the work of the Commissioners, Wilmot pointed out that his reports already numbered 246 large folio volumes. The Papers of Daniel Parker Coke, who resigned from the Commission in 1785, confirm the detailed work that the Commissioners were doing. But in fact only 400 out of some 5000 claimants had then been examined. In the debates in the House of Commons in July 1786, the difficulties of the exercise emerged. What had begun as an act of grace towards a few exiles in London had now become heavily involved in the terms of the Treaty, whereby the obligation was in some measure shifted to the American states. The problem was complicated by issues like losses sustained by enemy action, losses due to depreciation of money, losses due to American debts, all of which the Commissioners had agreed to ignore two years before; and they now fully accepted that they had to include in their estimates both loss of office and loss of professional income, suffered as a result of loyalty to the Crown. Moreover, in 1782 it had still been possible to believe that the Loyalist exiles would ultimately return to America; by 1785 few of them were prepared to do so, though a few gallant men like Samuel Curwen did. So the emphasis changed from being an economy probe into a small number of claims into a large-scale enquiry into a vast number of claimants, whose numbers steadily grew. At first the percentage that was granted was not fixed, but later Pitt's plan was adopted which fixed by schedule the percentage of approved losses to be paid, giving greater consideration to the small losers than the great. By the twelfth and final report of the British Commissioners, 15 May 1789, Wilmot, who stayed on the post to the end, said that they had in all received 3225 claims and examined 2291, that the total demand on the exchequer was £8 026 045 and the amount awarded was £3 292 452, almost 100 times as much as was being distributed in 1782. If, to the compensation in money, we add the cost of establishing the Loyalists in Nova Scotia and Canada, the total amount expended by the British government for their American adherents was at least 7 million pounds. So much for the attempt of the Government in the 1780s to impose economy on public expenditure.[11]

To the historian the value of the evidence is not merely financial but social. A great many first impressions come through. First and repeatedly, of course, is the story of human suffering and human anguish. This is particularly so where the claimants are women. Thus when Mrs Elizabeth Ivey of Rhode Island reached the Scilly Isles even the ship on which she was a passenger was shipwrecked; she staggered ashore, herself heavily pregnant, after witnessing the drowning of her husband and two sons; all she had in the world were the soaking clothes she was wearing. Daniel Leonard could point out that one of the reasons why he wrote so bitterly as *Massachusettensis* was that as a known Loyalist in Boston the mob had fired into his bedroom in August 1774 at a time when his wife was in childbirth, with the consequence that the child was born an idiot. In 1780 he got a bounty of £560 a year and became Chief Justice of Bermuda. Or consider the case of Mrs Christian Amiel. She was 67 and she claimed that none of her six sons could help her, because they were all grown up and were not with her. In fact their names are a roll-call of loyalism; John was a Major of

Brigade with the 6oth Regiment, Peter a Lieutenant of Marines, Robert a Lieutenant in the 17th Regiment and trying to live off his pay, Henry an ensign in the 22nd Regiment of Foot, stationed at Windsor, Otto, formerly in the 17th Foot, had sold out and was seeking his fortune in the West Indies, and Philip lately a midshipman was Master of a vessel bound for the West Indies and struggling to earn a living. In other words we have a picture of a break up of a family, once affluent, and no doubt as officers seeking to keep up appearances, but all totally dispersed by the war. The documents are rich with many such human stories.

It is very striking how many of the claimants are ministers of religion, many of whom were able to find parishes in Britain. And it is equally striking that quite a number of the black claimants assert that they are free blacks, though not all had their claims allowed. Official reading indeed would suggest that most of the blacks who were liberated were already, or claimed to be, free men, e.g. Thomas Johnstone, John Twine, who swore he was born a free man but could not prove even his own age, and Ben Whitcuff, who claimed to have been employed as a spy by Clinton and to have been hanged at Cranbury in New Jersey. He had been hanging only three minutes when an obliging party of the 5th Regiment came by and cut him down. He got 15 guineas—compensation apparently for surviving.

Secondly, there are, of course a few exotics among the claimants, though it should be noted that only nine claimants were declared by the Commissioners to be frauds. One of these was Ferdinand Smith, or Smyth, who afterwards added the name of Stuart and claimed to be the great grandson of Charles II. He had in his own phrase 'been bred to physic' at one of the Scottish Universities though he did not name it, and he had practised medicine, he claimed, in New Kent County, Virginia, earning £600 a year. He said that he had raised the Royal Hunters—185 men at his own expense—but he brought some serious charges against Colonel Simcoe. He had been appointed a Captain of the Queens Rangers by Sir William Howe in 1777, and he claimed to be an owner of estates in at least three different places. Under examination however it became clear that he had gone out in fact as an indentured servant, and witnesses used phrases like 'he was a man worth nothing', 'his character was such in the country that I would not have trusted him with a shilling', and of the claim that he was a Doctor, this 'was a joke amongst the neighbours'. He got nothing from the Commission.

Thirdly, the group in London included some distinguished names, Sewall, Hutchinson, Vassall, Loring, and, from New York, DeLancey, Cruger, and William Bayard. Bayard is in fact an example of the demands being made on the Government from those who might be thought able to meet their own losses. Bayard had been a delegate from New York to the Continental Congress, but in 1776 he became a Loyalist and helped to raise the Orange Rangers in New York. He got an allowance from the Government of £200 a year from 1779 onwards, but in the same year returned to New York as agent for prizes and got a 5 per cent commission on each prize that was brought in. It was estimated by 1783 that he had made £24 000 in New York currency during the war—approximately £13 500 sterling. When he died in 1804 it was at his stately seat, Greenwich House near Southampton. Similarly his brother Robert earned £20 000 sterling as a Judge of the Admiralty Court in New York, and lived 'in a very gentle and Handsome manner'. But both claimed for their losses. So, for that matter, did Joseph Galloway, who in his evidence to the Commission pointed out that as his interest in politics developed in the early 70s he had greatly reduced his law practice. As a speaker of the assembly he was paid £200 a year, and he claimed that his professional services had earned him a further £2000 a year; but his claim for losses of professional earnings was rejected. There was justice here, for when the British were in Philadelphia he had got £300 a year as a magistrate and another £770 as Superintendent of the Port. It is interesting to note that Sir William Howe, whom Galloway cited as a witness in his favour, said of him, on 1 February 1784, that he had no doubt about Galloway's loyalty or his wishes to promote the King's Service, but he did not believe that 'his heart was materially concerned in it'. The striking feature about this colonial aristocracy is that they were overwhelmingly from the North and Middle colonies; there seems little evidence of an influx of Loyalists from the South before the evacuation of Charleston. But equally this aristocracy were demanding, and went on being so. As late as 1790 both the Fairfax family and the Penns were making very heavy claims for losses themselves. Fairfax in the end got £60 000 compensation, and the Penns, who claimed almost 1 million pounds got half a million. Governor Bull got £500 per annum; so did Oliver de Lancey; James de Lancey £200 per annum; Professor John Vardell, Professor of Divinity at the College of New York, £500. On the other hand Thomas Boylston, the merchant, found himself still in Newgate Jail in 1793.

Fourthly, there are some interesting revelations here of the earning power of professional classes in the late colonial period, especially lawyers and doctors. Thomas Pephoe of Charleston, a lawyer, claimed to be earning between £1000 and £2000 a year when the revolution broke out. Brigadier-General Skinner, the attorney general of New Jersey, estimated his earnings at one thousand pounds per year. Dr Nathaniel Perkins of Boston claimed to make profits of £600 a year from his medical practice in the City, and a further £100 from visits to patients outside it. He charged 3s. a visit and 6s. if he was called in as a consultant. The Rev. Jacob Duché, who had the united charge of Christ Church and St Peter's in Philadelphia, earned £600 a year, but his application for aid was not treated with much sympathy. He had become a Whig and indeed had been chaplain to the Continental Congress. But he found revolutionary violence and separation from England not to his taste. Member of an old Philadelphia family, brother-in-law to Frances Hopkinson, he had studied at Cambridge University and formed sentimental ties with the Mother Country. When Howe captured Philadelphia and promptly put him in jail, he experienced a decisive change of mind, and wrote to Washington urging him to abandon the cause. His brother-in-law blamed it all on the weakness of his nerves. His own way of putting it was that he had resigned his charge because of ill-health, but it did not stop him claiming for compensation nor did it prevent his ultimate return to Philadelphia in 1790. He ended up as a convert to Swedenborgianism. But it is at least clear that the professional classes could earn high salaries, and had an infinite capacity for 'perks'.

Even if it could be agreed that compensation was for 'loyalty', how could a Loyalist's loss of all that he might have made, be assessed, especially as in the eighteenth century so much could quite legitimately be made 'on the side?' Thus Abijah Willard undertook after Bunker Hill to supply the King's troops with provisions. When he was cross-examined about any omissions from his claim, he said that only his restraint had stopped him making an extra £20 000 out of the job, because the provision of hides and tallows were his 'perks'; and he had, out of his generosity, put every penny from this into the Government's purse.

Fifthly, the fundamental problem and the most tragic, is of the host of smaller fry who went with the tides of war. The Commission took a clear line that only Loyalists were to be rewarded, but who was a Loyalist? What about the late, but the genuine, converts? Moreover there were many, certainly in the Middle colonies and the South, who at the beginning simply assumed that Britain would win, and therefore were loyal from convention rather than conviction. Where did the true merit of loyalism lie? The commission in fact did not look very closely into human motivation; so long as their actions were correct, men had to be given the benefit of the doubt. Moreover, many claimed that they had taken patriot oaths without being really false to the King. If rebels were rebels, oaths taken to them—it was contended—need not be treated very seriously. 'The imposer of the oath 'tis breaks it; Not he who for convenience takes it'—Hudibras, as quoted by Samuel Curwen; although in such an argument there was more often sophistry and weakness than truth. But there is some evidence that Governor Tryon encouraged some dedicated Loyalists to call themselves rebels in order to act as spies, and this made the Commission's task particularly difficult.

Clearly the ordinary man was living in extraordinary times. Consider the case of Harrison Gray Jr, who said he left America because of his health in 1775, and who, says S. E. Morison, lived 'a grumbling existence in London', with a small pension from the government and a little American property that his nephew Harrison Gray Otis had saved from his father's estate. His father was Treasurer of the province and he was in name deputy Treasurer, for which office, he said, he had received £100 a year. But in fact the office of Deputy/Treasurer was his father's creation, and he got no direct pay from the province itself. John Chandler, who was one of the frankest of the Commission witnesses, said bluntly in his evidence that nothing ailed Harrison Gray—'he came away from fear of being killed'.

It is clear that the ordinary man, and still more the ordinary woman, suffered actuely from the war and at the end of the day was fortunate if a third of his claim was met. Moreover, whatever he got came years later and after great anguish. Samuel Curwen's account to the Reverend Isaac Smith of the impact of the sharp economy drive of 1783 is moving reading:

London, February 14 1783
Dear Sir...This day I went to the Treasury to inquire about my allowance, and to my comfort found it stood as at first. A few are raised, some struck off, more lessened. Of those that have come to my knowledge, Go. Oliver's is lessened £100, out of £300. Mr. Williams, who has married a fortune here, is struck off; Harrison Gray, with a wife and two children, struck off; his brother lessened to £50; D. Ingersoll reduced from £200 to £100; Samuel H. Sparhawk, from £150 to £80; Benjamin Gridley from £150 to £100; Thomas Danforth's, Samuel Sewall's, Samuel Porter's, Peter Johonnot's, G. Brinely's, Edward Oxnard's and mine continue as at first; Chandler's raised £50; Samuel Fitch's £20; Col. Morrow's £50; one whose name I forget is sunk from £100 to £30; and many names and sums totally forgotten. On the whole, it is said the sum paid last year to refugees, amounting to near £80,000, is now shrunk from the late reform to £38,000; and if the Commissioners act on the same frugal plan respecting the petitioners whose cases will probably soon be considered, I very much doubt whether the sum of last year's expenditures under this head, including all their additional allowances, will exceed this year's.

And sixthly, the records are equally interesting on the cities in which the exiles lived. They found London expensive, inhospitable, and very cold. 'This huge unwieldy town swarms with Americans grumbling and discontented', said J. H. Cruger, 'Of all countries in the world', said Harvard graduate Ward Chipman, 'this is the worst to be in without a good deal of money.' Curwen wrote to the Rev. Thomas Barnard:

Dear Sir,

The dissipation, self-forgetfulness and vicious indulgences of every kind which characterize this metropolis are not to be wondered at. The temptations are too great for that degree of philosophy and religion ordinarily possessed by the bulk of mankind. The unbounded riches of many afford the means of every species of luxury, which (thank God), our part of America is ignorant of; and the example of the wealthy and great is contagious.

And Curwen complained of the officiousness that delayed a visit to the British Museum by two or three weeks.

The chills and gloom were such that Dr John Jeffries found medicine more rewarding in London than he had in Boston. But he was interested even more in pioneer ballooning. He crossed the Channel in 1785 with Blanchard in a balloon. In the course of the voyage they found themselves descending much too rapidly and dropping into the Channel, and they had to jettison everything including the clothing they were wearing. Even this did not seem to avert disaster, so the heroes, remembering that they had drunk too much at breakfast, 'relieved their vehicle of 5 or 6 pounds more'. They landed safely, though they do not record the surprise of the welcoming party at their nakedness. As *The Harvard Alumni Bulletin* put it, 'the hero dined at Dover and went to France for tea'.

But in fact the Loyalists were alarmed to find themselves the reverse of heroes, with the exception of Hutchinson, Galloway and Chief Joseph Brandt of the Mohawk Indians. Many British radicals, large sections of the working class and even sympathizers like Boswell were quick to criticize them. Governor Hutchinson died in 1780 shortly after being publicly attacked in a speech by Charles James Fox—'that firebrand and source of American disputes'. Oxnard, like Benjamin Franklin before him, found England a land 'of liberty and pride'. Despite the conviviality of the New England Coffee house in Threadneedle Street, or the Jerusalem Tavern and St Clement's Coffee House, despite Samuel Curwen's weekly dinners at the Adelphi in the Strand, despite the fame in London of the American painters— John Singleton Copley and Benjamin West—the Loyalists found London far from congenial. If there was one city that they made their own it was Bristol, and by 1780 some distinguished Massachusetts figures were living there—Curwen, Oliver, Sewall, Faneuil and Coffin. Bristol was, of course, identified with the American cause, not only through Edmund Burke but by the presence in the House of Commons of its other member of Parliament—Henry Cruger, younger brother of J. H. Bristol is clearly an area where much more research into the Loyalists has to be done.

At the end of the day the British Government honoured the claims up to about one-third of the sum demanded; and of those receiving compensation, 941 or more than one-third were from New York, 321 from S. Carolina, 226 from Massachusetts, 200 from New Jersey, 148 from Pennsylvania, 140 from Virginia, 135 from N. Carolina and 129 from Georgia. Colonial officials were pensioned off; some got jobs in Britain or abroad. Ministers were found parishes. Those who had served in the Army went on to half-pay. And some on half-pay, like the colourful Benjamin Thompson, Count Rumford, went on receiving it when they were serving the state of Bavaria. 204 got pensions for loss of office totalling £26 000 per annum; another 588, who had lost no property but had other claims on government bounty, got annual allowances. Only 18 got more than £200 a year. Far more important were the arrangements made for the refugees who fled to Canada—Nova Scotia, New Brunswick and Upper Canada or Ontario. Here the British government was not only generous but farsighted. It granted 500 acres of land to heads of families, and 300 acres to single men; it set aside 2000 acres in each township to the support of religion and 1000 acres to the support of schools; it provided rations, fuel, clothing and other forms of assistance for a period of years. Altogether the government gave some 3 000 000 acres of land to the United Empire Loyalists, as they came to be called, and spent some $9 000 000 on resettling them.

Finally, it seems clear that two-thirds of the Loyalists were not natives. Many arrived in the colonies during the Seven Years War as members of the armed forces, which inculcated loyalty. And normally, the more recent an immigrant the greater the chance of loyalty. He usually had not done as well as the longer-established immigrants, he lacked their confidence, he had stronger ties with the homeland, and generally he felt more in need of a friend in the form of the British Government. Thus many Pennsylvania Loyalists were immigrants, the majority being comparatively recent arrivals. The great Loyalist strength in Georgia is certainly partly explained by the colony's high proportion (the highest of any colony) of immigrants. Many Germans were immigrant Loyalists. They undoubtedly shared the immigrant's desire for protection, and many felt gratitude to the British Government, which had sometimes paid their passage and granted them title to land that they now feared to lose. But ignorance of the English language compounded a general ignorance of the Revolutionary issues, and the majority of Germans remained neutral or Whig and were swept along by events in which they had little part. Many Scots were Loyalists also, and indeed usually bitterly unpopular. Some of them were factors at the ports, and had the reputation of being all too canny business men. Some were merchants connected with firms in Glasgow or London, a few were Indian traders, and others were demobilized soldiers, such as Allan McDonald, husband of the almost mythical Flora MacDonald. Many were Highlanders, often recently arrived in the New World. It may seem strange that many of these Highlanders, who had fought the House of Hanover in the 1745 rebellion and remembered the defeat of 1715, should prove such staunch Loyalists. But they wanted to avoid being three-time losers (in vain, as it turned out), and, furthermore, they had been well treated and given land in America, taking oaths of allegiance in the process. Remaining clannish, the Highlanders followed their leaders, and their leaders were generally loyal. The clan system was also a ready-made form of political organization, and it was organization that most Loyalists fatally lacked.

Other Highlanders came from Argyllshire, where the Campbells, traditionally loyal to the English monarchy, held sway. Thus George Campbell recounted that his relatives had been loyal during the 'Fifteen' and the 'Forty-Five', in which latter affray he himself had served as a youthful combatant. In 1774 Campbell emigrated to Philadelphia. There an old friend, 'whose Ancestors had been Dependents upon this Memorialist's Family, but who had emigrated in his Youth, and by his own Industry had accumulated a Fortune', tried to persuade Campbell to join the rebels, and he was offered command of a regiment. Campbell, however, said he preferred 'his hereditary Loyalty to every consideration of Interest'.

William H. Nelson has suggested that the various Loyalist groups were usually 'cultural minorities' in need of British help or protection, and fearful of an increase in the power of the majority. This theory is undoubtedly valuable. As Nelson points out, the Dutch and the Germans were Tory mainly where they had not been Anglicized, and New Rochelle, the only place where the French Calvinists still spoke French, seems to have been the one area of substantial Huguenot Loyalism. One can add such examples as the small farmers of New York who had rebelled under Prendergast against their Whig landlords; the Highland Catholic tenants of Sir John Johnson; the Baptists of Ashfield, Massachusetts, who were struggling against the established Congregational Church, as were the Sandemanians in Massachusetts and Connecticut. In other words, the Tory in 1776, as at other periods in American history, was apt to be an enemy because he was and felt himself to be an alien.[12]

There is much to be done also in tracing their subsequent careers, from Bavarian Counts like Rumford to cross-channel balloonists like Jeffries. I have said nothing on the American side of the story, the persecution, the loyalty oaths, the varying attitudes of the different states after 1783. A few risked the return, like Samuel Curwen. In his *Journal*, he writes:

Sept. 25. Arrived at Boston, and at half past three o'clock landed at the end of Long Wharf, after an absence of nine years and five months, occasioned by a lamented civil war, excited by ambitious, selfish men here and in England, to the disgrace, dishonour, distress and disparagement of these extensive territories. By plunder and rapine some few have accumulated wealth, but many more are greatly injured in their circumstances; some have to lament over the wreck of their departed wealth and estates, of which pitiable number I am; my affairs having sunk into irretrievable ruin.

To sum up, the central fact remains that in 1776 there were no 'Loyalists' outside Washington's army, nor a lot of Patriots either. Even as early as 1775 many later Loyalists were still good Whigs. What existed in 1776 was a rebel army which it was

Howe's task to destroy with as little civil fuss and fury as possible. Howe was right to assume that to destroy the army was to end the rebellion; those not in arms, he assumed, were law-abiding colonists, then loyal if not loyalist. By 1778, and in part by British and Hessian looting, but only in part for that reason, there was a nation in rebellion; a nation, which in part because of French intervention, but only in part for that reason, could now see a chance of total victory, with a continent, if necessary, in which to sit out time. Those who by 1778 were Loyalist were thus of a different order—and suffered a different fate—from that majority of the colonists who two years before had been neutral, passive and therefore, 'loyal'. The study of Loyalism in these crucial seven years, is thus in a sense a study in semantics as much as in strategy, and it needs to be tackled in depth and against a British as well as an American background. It is probably the most important aspect of the Revolution still to be tackled. And until it is tackled definitely—and its lessons understood—we shall fail to grasp that since 1776 all wars have been at once both civil and ideological struggles. In the tensions and tragedies of the Loyalists, as in the tensions and tragedies of Dixie, America had its own moments of truth. As Dr Evans has shown, a study of the Loyalists can be used to reveal problems of loyalty, of where duty lies. This is a recurring challenge for Americans, from Bunker Hill to Saigon. For the Loyalists were honest and decent men, as were the Patriots, with a code quite as true.

John Eardley-Wilmot began his enquiry with some distaste for the Loyalists. In the end he came to admire their dedication and their devotion. His account of the Claims Commission proceedings, published in 1815, was prefaced with Milton's words:

> Their Loyalty they kept, their love, their zeal,
> Nor number, nor example with them wrought
> To swerve from truth, or change their constant mind.

They have been called men without a country. Theirs was a greater tragedy: they were men of two countries, uncertain which was home. Jonathan Sewall reported that Samuel Porter (Harvard, class of 1763) was physically ill with melancholy—

and Thomas Hutchinson wrote 'I would rather die in a little country farmhouse in New England than in the best gentleman's seat in old England.' And Frederick Philipse of Tarrytown on Hudson—'Fred III'—died in Chester, England, in 1788, landless, broken, and blind. A petition from several Charleston, South Carolina, Loyalists said: 'Although your Memorialists differ from their fellow Citizens in political opinion, they all have and ever shall retain a natural affection for the Country where they have passed their happiest days and have their dearest connexions.'

On 29 March 1783, Major Walter Dulany, of the Maryland Loyalists, wrote to the commander-in-chief in New York, Sir Guy Carleton, about the prospect of being given a permanent commission, explaining his position thus:

My duty as a subject; the happiness which America enjoyed under the British government; and the miseries to which she would be reduced by an independance; were the motives that induced me to join the British Army; nor are there any dangers, or difficulties that I would not cheerfully undergo, to effect a happy restoration.

But, at the same time, that I acted, with the greatest zeal, against my rebellious countrymen I never forget that I was an American— If therefore, Sir, Independence should be granted, and the war still continued, I should deem it extremely improper to remain in a situation, obliging me to act either directly or indirectly against America.

The Loyalists, we should remind ourselves, were Americans too. They just guessed wrong. And in history, as in politics, as in life, you have to be on the winning side.

NOTES

1. William H. Nelson, *The American Tory*, Oxford, 1961.

Jackson T. Main, *Rebel versus Tory, the Crisis of the Revolution 1773–1776*, Chicago, 1963, p. 1.

Thomas Hutchinson, *The History of the Colony and Province of Massachusetts Bay*, ed. Lawrence S. Mayo, Cambridge, Mass., 1936, III, p. 75.

Samuel Curwen, *Journal and Letters 1775–1748*, ed. S. A. Ward, New York, 1842, p. 409.

Jonathan Boucher, *Reminiscences of an American Loyalist 1738–1789*, Boston, New York, 1925.

Joseph Galloway, *The Claim of the American Loyalists*, London, 1788.

George Chalmers, *Political Annals of the Present United Colonies*, London, 1780.

Daniel Leonard, *Novanglus and Massachusettensis*, New York, 1968.

David Ramsay, *History of the American Revolution*, 2 vols, London, 1793.

Alexander Graydon, *Memoirs of a Life, Chiefly Passed in Pennsylvania, within the Last Sixty Years*, Harrisburg, 1811.

Charles Stedman, *The History of the Origin, Progress and Termination of the American War*, 2 vols, London, 1794.

2. The figures of 100 000 are those of Phineas Bond, *Letters of Phineas Bond*, American Historical Association, *Annual Report 1896*, 2 vols, Washington, 1897, I, 648.

M. C. Tyler, 'The Party of the Loyalists', *A.H.R.* I, No. 1, October 1895, p. 31.

R. R. Palmer, *The Age of the Democratic Revolution*, Princeton, 1959, p. 188.

3. H. E. Egerton (ed.), *The Royal Commission on the Losses and Services of the American Loyalists 1783–1785*, Oxford, 1915.

4. C. Vann Woodward, 'The Irony of Southern History' in *The Burden of Southern History*, Baton Rouge, 1960, pp. 167–91.

B. J. Crick and M. Alman, *A Guide to Manuscripts relating to America in Great Britain and Ireland*, London, 1961.

Elisha Hutchinson to his wife, Egerton Mss, British Museum 2669, f. 60.

5. Hutchinson, op. cit.; Audit Office Papers (P.R.O.) Series 12 and 13 *passim*.

6. Egerton, op. cit.; Mary Beth Norton, *The British Americans, the Loyalist exiles in England, 1774–1789*, Boston, 1972.

Andrew Oliver (ed.), *Journal of Samuel Curwen, Loyalist*, Harvard University Press, 1972.

Lawrence Gipson, *The British Empire Before the American Revolution*, New York, 15 vols, 1936–70.

7. Lorenzo Sabine, *Biographical Sketches of Loyalists of the American Revolution with a Historical Essay*, Boston, 2 vols, 1864.

Moses C. Tyler, *Literary History of the American Revolution 1763–1783*, 2 vols, New York, 1897; 'The Party of the Loyalists', op. cit.

C. Van Tyne, *The Loyalists in the American Revolution 1776–1783*, New York, 1902.

8. James Stark, *The Loyalists of Massachusetts*, Boston, 1910.

Otis Hammond, 'Tories of New Hampshire in the War of the Revolution', *New Hampshire Historical Society Publications* 5, 1917.

Edward Jones, *The Loyalists of New Jersey, Collections of the New Jersey Historical Society X*, 1927.

Isaac Harrell, *Loyalism in Virginia*, Durham, 1926.

L. H. Gibson, *Jared Ingersoll*, New Haven, 1920; '*Proceedings* of Commissioners on Loyalist Claims', Ontario Bureau of Archives *Second Report*, Ottawa, 2 vols, 1905; Coke, see Egerton (ed.), op. cit.

Wilbur Siebert, 'American Loyalists in Eastern Quebec', Royal Society of Canada *Transactions*, VII, 1913; 'The Legacy of the American Revolution to the British West Indies', Ohio State University *Bulletin*, XVII, 1913; 'Loyalist Settlements on Gaspe', Royal Society of Canada *Transactions*, VIII, 1914; 'The Exodus of Loyalists from Penobscot', Ohio State University *Bulletin*, XVIII, 1914; 'The Dispersion of American Tories', *Mississippi Valley Historical Review*, I, 1914; 'Loyalists in the Niagara Peninsula', Royal Society of Canada *Transactions*, IX, 1915; 'Loyalist Refugees of New Hampshire', Ohio State University *Bulletin*, XXI, 1916; 'Refugee Loyalists in Connecticut', Royal Society of Canada *Transactions*, X, 1916;

'Loyalists in West Florida', *Mississippi Valley Historical Review*, II, 1916; 'Loyalists of Pennsylvania', Ohio State University *Bulletin*, XXIV, 1920; 'Kentucky's Struggle', *Mississippi Valley Historical Review*, VII, 1920; 'Loyalist Troops of New England', *New England Quarterly*, IV, 1931.

Boucher, op. cit.

Alexander Chesney, *Journal*, Ohio State University *Bulletin*, XXVI, 1921, No. 4.

Ann Hutton, *Letters of a Loyalist Lady*, London, 1927.

Samuel Seabury, *Letters of a Westchester Farmer*, ed. C. H. Vance, Westchester County Historical Society *Publications*, VIII, 1930.

9. To these should now be added Robert Calhoon's splendid survey, *The Loyalists in Revolutionary America, 1760–1781*, New York, 1973, which appeared after this paper was delivered.

For a survey of recent Loyalist writing see Wallace Brown, 'The View at Two Hundred Years: The Loyalists of the American Revolution', *American Antiquarian Society Proceedings*, LXXX, April 1970, 25–47.

10. Paul H. Smith, *Loyalists and Recoats, a study in revolutionary British policy*, Chapel Hill, 1964.

Piers Mackesy, *The War for America, 1775–1783*, London, 1964. Audit Office, series 12 and 13 *passim*; Colonial Office Papers series 5.

George Reese (ed.), *The Cornwallis Papers*, Virginia Independence Bicentennial Commission, 1970.

11. M. B. Norton, op. cit., Chapter 7.

Wallace Brown, *The King's Friends*, Providence, 1965.

J. Eardley-Wilmot, *Historical View of the Commission for Enquiring into the Losses Services and Claims of the American Loyalists*, London, 1815.

Eugene R. Fingerhut, 'Uses and Abuses of the American Loyalist claims: a Critique of Quantitative Analyses', *William and Mary Quarterly*, 3rd series, XXV April 1968, pp. 245–58.

12. A.O. 12 and 13, *passim*; C.O. 5, *passim*.

Ian C. C. Graham, *Colonists from Scotland: Emigration to North America 1707–83*, Ithaca, New York, 1956.

Richard S. Hooker (ed.), *The Carolina Back-Country on the Eve of the Revolution: the Journal and other writings of Charles Woodmason, Anglican Itinerant*, Chapel Hill, 1953.

Duane Meyer, *The Highland Scots of North Carolina, 1732–76*, Chapel Hill, 1957.

Some Case Studies in Revolutionary Loyalty

Franklin, John Adams and Jefferson

RALPH KETCHAM

Though the word 'loyalist' in considering the American Revolution is generally, and properly, applied to those who repudiated the Declaration of Independence and remained 'loyal' to the Crown, it is true as well that those who wrote and signed the Declaration were 'loyalists' of a sort. The three most important signers, for example, Benjamin Franklin, John Adams, and Thomas Jefferson, each began his life as a fervently loyal Briton and each remained as long as he lived a captive, in a sense, of British culture. Yet each was a rebel, a rejector of his home land. To manage this tension was often an excruciating experience, especially for men of culture and rich historical understanding. It was simply impossible for them to be fundamentally disloyal, that is to purge themselves of the habits, values, and attitudes essential to their very being—*English* habits, values, and attitudes they thought—yet they declared themselves *independent* of Britain. The careers of Franklin, Adams, and Jefferson help us measure the nature and consequences of this traumatic tension.

The trauma over loyalty, in fact, as we see it in the minds of these three men, is part of a larger pattern that carries well into the early national period. Three rough stages can be observed: First, most explicitly, men had to *declare* themselves no-longer-Britons. This is the 'revolution in the minds and hearts of the people' John Adams asserted 'was effected before the war commenced'—a casting off of national loyalty. It was precisely this, of course, that those we call Loyalists could not do. Second, shorn of one national allegiance, the revolutionists had to form another one as best they could. They began to do this in the

Declaration of Independence, continued it earnestly, if un-evenly, in adopting the state constitutions, and largely con-cluded it as they implemented the federal constitution of 1787. But, these declarations and forms of government were mere skeleton, bones without the flesh and blood that gave a nation life and meaning. What was the *character* of the new nation to be? What peculiar qualities and attitudes would give the new United States a distinctiveness akin to that of the ancient nations from Japan to Ireland and from Russia to Ethiopia? What would its people be like? What conceptions of good character, economic growth, aesthetics, and relation to the environment, would guide national development? It was this sense of incompleteness that let another signer of the Declara-tion of Independence, Dr Benjamin Rush, to assert in 1785 that far from being over, the American Revolution had just begun. 'We have changed our forms of government', Rush wrote the English radical Richard Price, 'but it remains yet to effect a revolution in our principles, opinions, and manners, so as to accommodate them to the forms of government we have adop-ted.'[1] The statements of Adams that in 1775 the revolution had been accomplished and of Rush that in 1785 it had just begun, are, of course, complementary, not contradictory. Adams noted a climax of one phase of the revolution, while Rush saw that another phase was only in its early stages.

This broad framework, then, of a psychic and intellectual revolution extending from, say, 1750 when Britons on the western side of the Atlantic were by and large super patriots to, say, 1820 when the national character had asserted itself, helps us to see how the loyalties of Franklin, Adams, and Jefferson differed from those of their erstwhile compatriots who remained loyal to Britain.

II

Though Benjamin Franklin has become, through the *persona* of Poor Richard and the vividness of his *Autobiography*, the arche-type American, his mind and character can also be seen as the fulfilment of a 'personality type' in development in England since the early days of the Reformation. We know, for example, of the growth in Tudor and Stuart England of a bourgeois class possessing attitudes of earnestness, self-help, hard work, upward mobility, and Puritan piety. Franklin's family, as he was proudly aware, came from this culture, which in England produced men like John Bunyan and Daniel Defoe, each remembered by Franklin as of cardinal significance in his early intellectual growth. Though Franklin and others stamped these qualities as 'American traits', they had received mature expression by English authors admired by Franklin, and they were solidly imbedded in a strand of English culture long before his birth.

In 1685, then, when Franklin's father emigrated to Boston, he brought with him a Puritan-bourgeois life style that, as thousands of other Britons were discovering, found a most congenial environment in the New World. At the same time the increasingly dominant spirit in England was that of the enterprising commercial classes, which, under Pitt's leadership, achieved the triumphs of the Great War for Empire. It was to this England, vigorous, expansive, Protestant, and progressive, that Franklin and other colonials gave such fierce devotion. They lived by its values, enjoyed its culture, thrived under its economics, and sustained its geopolitics. Whatever the difference between the Boston of Franklin's youth and the Philadelphia of his young manhood, as outposts of the British Empire they shared the hope and self-confidence (and arrogance) engendered by its dynamism.

In 1751 he expressed a vision of the future growth of North America which he held to the end. 'What an accession of Power to the British Empire by Sea as well by Land! What increase of trade and navigation! What numbers of ships and seamen!... In proportion to the increase of the Colonies, a vast demand is growing for British Manufactures, a glorious Market.' Britain to Franklin was 'a wise and good Mother' and the colonies growing children. Any act by either against the other, he observed, 'weakens the whole family'. He hoped at the same time that Pennsylvania would be settled by Britons, rather than 'Palatine Boors', who spread an alien culture, or by 'black and tawny' races. He was, he said, 'partial to the complexion of my country', meaning, of course, England.[2]

Franklin's Empire loyalty, though, was not at heart mere imperialism or bigotry. He believed in its growth because he thought that under the British flag free, self-reliant, and productive life would most flourish. The evidence of the despotic, stagnant French and Spanish colonies surrounding the rapidly growing English plantations was for Franklin and nearly all his compatriots vindication enough of the British system. He was always sure that the fertile Mississippi Valley should be settled by independent yeomen like those of Massachusetts and Pennsylvania. 'What a glorious thing it would be', he wrote George Whitefield in 1756, 'to settle in that fine Country a large Strong Body of Religious and Industrious People!' He recognized, too, that slavery had no place in the development he envisioned. Any man, black or white, kept in slavery would, since he did not 'benefit by his own Care or Diligence', be negligent, slothful, and dishonest. Furthermore, in addition to being oppressed and diseased themselves, slaves 'pejorated the families that used them; the white Children becoming proud, disgusted with Labour, and being educated in idleness are rendered unfit to get a Living by Industry.'[3] Nothing in short, more dominated Franklin's mind than his vision of the *kind* of people and the *kind* of settlement that should spread across the American West. Until he was sixty or more years old, he thought this possible *only* under the British flag.

Resistance within Pennsylvania to the privileges insisted upon by Proprietor Thomas Penn and his supporters called forth in 1756 a pointed statement of Franklin's political principles. 'The People of this Province', Franklin averred, 'are generally of the middling sort,...chiefly industrious Farmers, Artificers, or Men in Trade; they enjoy and are fond of Freedom, *and the meanest among them* thinks he has a right to Civility from the Greatest.' To protect this freedom, the people needed to elect their own legislative assembly, 'by private Ballot...[to] best show their free Inclination and Judgment'. In ridiculing the haughty, aristocratic airs of the Proprietary supporters who expected 'the middling sort' to 'stand cap-in-hand when they speak of the Lordings, and *your Honour* begins or ends every sentence',[4] Franklin showed again that a certain human dignity, a basic freedom, and even a measure of equality, had become indispensable to his conception of a just society. That he still supposed Britain to be a bulwark of this kind of society was underscored in 1757 when he 'went home' to England as agent for the Assembly to appeal to the British government for relief from the injustices of the Proprietor.

During eighteen years (1757–75) in England, Franklin lived in a remarkable laboratory for testing both his British loyalty and his American habits. Making his home in the city of Hume, Burke, and Dr Johnson, Franklin embraced the social and cultural life of London. The famous writers, scientists, and politicians whose deeds and words had filled Franklin's paper in Philadelphia were now his frequent companions. He attended meetings of the Royal Society, went to Westminster Abbey to hear Handel's *Messiah*, visited the country estate of Lord Kames, travelled on the continent with the Queen's physician, received an honorary degree from Oxford, joined a coffee house club of political liberals and otherwise enjoyed a society immensely richer and more cosmopolitan than any in the colonies. Nothing, he wrote in 1772, 'can be more agreable' than life in Britain. 'I seldom dine at home in winter, and could spend the whole summer in the countryhouses of inviting friends, if I chose it.' During a brief trip to America in 1763, he wrote sentimentally that 'of all the enviable things England has, I envy most its People...That little Island enjoys in almost every Neighborhood more sensible, virtuous Minds, than we can collect in ranging 100 Leagues of our vast Forests.'[5] To Franklin and other sophisticated colonials, primitive life had but limited appeal. Before they could throw off old loyalties or consider new ones, they had to think long and seriously about complexities of culture and nationality not easily acquired—or discarded.

Along with the delight in social life, Franklin found at first what he hoped would be entirely practical channels to work within British politics. The great Pitt understood American interests, he thought, and in both houses of Parliament there were 'many...who are Friends to Liberty and of Noble Spirits'. Franklin's strategy, then, as late as 1766, was to discourage 'Excesses' in America so that the enemies of colonial freedom might be 'disappointed', to support friendly Ministries, and to '*thereby effectually secure* the American Interest in Parliament'. Franklin's loyal predisposition, initially at least, caused him to underestimate the machinations of British politics hostile or indifferent to American interests.

His education in realities soon began, however. He had not been in England a month before he heard from Lord Granville himself the 'alarming' doctrine that '*the King is the Legislator of the Colonies*' and that his instructions 'so far as relates to [the colonies are] the *Law of the Land*'. The other dominating member of the Privy Council was 'for carrying the [Royal] Prerogative higher in all Respects' even in Britain. Hence, Franklin observed glumly, 'one may easily conjecture what Reception a Petition concerning Privileges from the Colonies may meet from those who are known to think even the People of England have too many'. Furthermore, Lord Halifax, President of the Board of Trade, had fathered one 'military Government for a Colony' and thought that arrangement proper for other restless plantations. Among these 'great People' who had the real power over the colonies, observed the knowledgeable Thomas Penn, 'Franklin's popularity is nothing...[and] he will be looked very coldly upon', whatever his fame among 'electricians', moralists, and philosopher-statesmen.[6] Franklin gradually discovered that Penn was right and that the liberal currents of English thought so readily circulated to America, and the opinions of his enlightened friends, were far different from attitudes in the seats of power. Lords and bishops and magnates, seldom heard in Philadelphia, in London spoke loudly and acted decisively. To confront *this* England was for Franklin a traumatic and eventually transforming experience.

At the same time, like a good reporter of humble origins, Franklin observed the stark contrast between the British countryside and that in America.

I have recently made a Tour through Ireland and Scotland. [he wrote in 1772] In those Countries a small Part of the Society are Landlords, great Noblemen, and Gentlemen, extreamly opulent, living in the highest Affluence and Magnificence: The Bulk of the People Tenants extreamly poor, living in the most sordid Wretchedness, in dirty Hovels of Mud and Straw, and cloathed only in Rags.

I thought often of the Happiness of New England, where every

Man is a Freeholder, has a Vote in publick Affairs, lives in a tidy, warm House, has plenty of good Food and Fewel, with whole cloaths from Head to Foot, the Manufacture perhaps of his own Family...But if they should ever envy the Trade of these Countries, I can put them in a Way to obtain a Share of it. Let them with three fourths of the People of Ireland live the Year round on Potatoes and Buttermilk, without Shirts, then may their Merchants export Beef, Butter, and Linnen. Let them, with the Generality of the Common People of Scotland, go Barefoot, them may they make large Exports of Shoes and Stockings: And if they will be content to wear Rags, like the Spinners, and Weavers of England, they may make Cloths and Stuffs for all Parts of the World.[7]

What, then happened to Franklin's national loyalty between 1750 and 1776? His lodestar throughout was his vision of the future of North America: hard-working, prosperous, self-governing yeomen spreading across and cultivating the Mississippi Valley, the same idea that transfixed every metaphysician of the American heartland from Jefferson to Frederick Jackson Turner. In Franklin's day the practical advantages as well as the emotional satisfactions of doing this under the British flag were great. England in the eighteenth century was, even her enemies agreed, the bastion of free government, obviously more fit than other nations to guide liberty-loving colonies. Furthermore, the Royal Navy was a matchless protector for exposed plantations far from home. Then, to a man proud of his culture and already part of the universal brotherhood of learning and science, retaining English practices, using English institutions, and communicating with English colleagues was the obvious way to keep contact with western civilization. Altogether, the conception of a many-membered family acting co-operatively to extend what Jefferson would call an 'Empire of Liberty' across the Atlantic and then across North America, was overwhelmingly attractive. As long as there seemed any prospect at all that this growth might take place within the British Empire, there was no reason even to think about the perils of a new national loyalty.

Then, as Franklin observed the life of ordinary people in Britain, and lived through the Stamp Act, the Townshend Duties, the tea tax, and all the rest, he adhered to the *substance* of both his vision of the future and his American life style, rather than to the *form* of his British allegiance. But, in willingly renouncing England, he *had* disinherited, and thereby probably diminished himself. Were Shakespeare and Milton, Drake and Wolfe still 'his' after he had foresworn allegiance to George III? In what relation did he stand to the land of his forefathers, he, the first Franklin who had ever thought for a moment about what his nationality was?

Winston Churchill has observed that the American colonists 'had no common national tradition except that against which they were revolting'.[8] They had, self-consciously at least, no indigenous culture like that a conquered people maintain against their overlords, nor did they rebel because they had been captured by the thought of the French *philosophes* or any other foreign ideology. If the colonials declared themselves to be no longer Britons, *what were they?* If they discarded the infinitude of customs, cadences, symbols, hardships, inflections, instincts, and reverences that for centuries had been England, what then? As the pre-revolutionary debates show on almost every page, the colonials often sidestepped this issue, at least until the Declaration of Independence, by proclaiming that they sought only the rights of Englishmen as they were understood not only by Patrick Henry and Sam Adams but by a host of men in Old England as well. Much of this claim was justified. Nonetheless, in withdrawing their allegiance from Britain, Franklin and his compatriots opened profound, perplexing questions that, as John Adams understood, even in the asking amounted to a revolution.

In France for nine years after 1776, Franklin sought to find in French culture replacements for his abandoned Englishness. In part he became the 'Enlightenment man' who could, as he told Tom Paine, say 'where liberty is there is my country'. When he and Voltaire met in the moving scene at the French Academy, the cry went up, 'how enchanting to see Solon and Sophocles embracing!' Franklin also quickly accustomed himself to French Court life and became the lion of Parisian society. All this, one feels sure, by way of filling the gap left by his rejection of the English culture he had so much enjoyed for two decades. He also was quick to see that French power and French sponsorship were necessary if the new nation was to survive amid the anarchy of international politics. In fact, for Franklin, as for Adams and Jefferson, living in France provided a perspective on 'national character' which deepened sensitivity for the essentials of American character.

Exposure to French culture, though, very soon persuaded Franklin that the ways of life in the New World were at least as far from the ways of Paris as from those of London. Though *Poor Richard* was immensely popular in France and the *philosophes* saw Franklin as an archetype man of the New World, there was in fact very little about every day life in the realm of Louis XVI for Philadelphia's first citizen to admire. Random events revealed the old diplomat's New-World partialities. Geneva was the only French-speaking city he thought uncorrupted and virtuous enough to be safe for his grandson's education—protestant, republican Geneva was much more to Franklin's taste than opulent, decadent Versailles. He admonished his daughter to be content with Pennsylvania home spun when she requested some elegant French lace. He thought the descent of titles in families as absurd as hereditary professors of mathematics, suggesting instead 'ascending honor for parents of worthy persons'. He objected to making the bald eagle the national symbol of the new nation because he 'does not get his living honestly...He watches the labour of the Fishing-Hawk, and, when that diligent Bird has at length taken a Fish...the Bald Eagle pursues him, and takes it from him.' The turkey, Franklin proposed instead, would be a better national symbol. He was 'not only native to America, but as well useful, industrious, and courageous'.[9]

Most revealing, though, of the life style Franklin hoped to encourage in the new world was his 'Information to those who would remove to America', written in 1782 in response to many applications from Europeans who supposed that in America 'there are...an abundance of profitable offices to be disposed of, which the Natives are not qualified to fill; and that, having few Persons of Family among them, Strangers of Birth must be greatly respected, and easily obtain the best of those Offices, which will make all their Fortunes'. In America, Franklin said, remembering his own runaway arrival in Philadelphia without friends or money, 'People do not inquire concerning a Stranger *What is he?* but, *What can he do?* If he has any useful Art, he is welcome, and if he exercises it, and behaves well, he will be respected by all that know him; but a mere Man of Quality, who, on that Account, wants to live upon the Public, by some Office or Salary, will be despised and disregarded'. Who should come to America, then? 'Hearty young Labouring Men' willing to carve a farm from the wilderness, 'tolerably good workmen in any of the Mechanic Arts', and even 'Persons of Moderate Fortunes and Capitals' who sought a country where their children would have abundant opportunity. 'Multitudes of poor People from England, Ireland, Scotland, and Germany', Franklin pointed out, had 'in a few years become wealthy Farmers, who, in their own countries...could never have emerged from the poor Condition wherein they were born.' Apprenticeships where masters trained young men in a trade and taught them to 'read, write, and cast accounts', were readily obtainable even by ignorant immigrants just off the ship. 'If they are proof', he noted in capsulating what he hoped would become the 'meaning' of America in the world, 'they begin first as Servants or Journeymen; and if they are sober, industrious, and frugal, they soon become Masters, establish themselves in Business, marry, raise Families, and become respectable Citizens.'[10]

Franklin thus pointed out what he was to put more personally in his *Autobiography*. The character or meaning of the new United States was to be found in the values, habits, and opportunities of its common people. Rather than taking pride in a glittering court, or a grand empire, or dynastic ambition, or even the glories that had made Athens or Florence famous, the qualities traditionally associated with national purpose or character, the United States would invite assessment, for better or for worse, according to the way of life of its ordinary citizens. Instead of fame for the glamour of its princesses, the beauty of its statuary, the courage of its soldiers, or the piety of its priests, the new world nation would be renowned he hoped, for the use by its citizens of the virtues taught by Poor Richard to improve their daily lives. This way of life, in the final analysis, engaged his deepest loyalty, and a reluctant conviction that

British rule would stunt it, caused his repudiation of a seventy-year-old loyalty to the British crown.

III

Some of the same changing loyalty and settlement of convictions are evident in the career of John Adams. Though he was of the fifth generation of his family to live in Braintree, Massachusetts, and he proudly told George III in 1785 that he knew nothing of any English relatives, he was grown to manhood before it ever occurred to him that he might be any less an Englishman than a resident of Bristol or Yorkshire. To him, to be English was no mere pledge of allegiance; it was to have a purpose, to revere a tradition, to possess a culture, indeed, it was life itself. Furthermore, his Christian education taught him that that nation, which had defeated the Spanish Armada and humbled the armies of Louis XIV, was the defender of the Reformation against the superstitions and tyranny of Rome. For a Puritan this was the central fact of 200 years of Western history. In living as pious yeomen in Braintree the Adamses supposed themselves to be fulfilling an entirely English life-style, destined, they hoped, to become characteristic for Britons on both sides of the Atlantic. The colony of Massachusetts, with relatively few non-British immigrants in 1750, felt itself peculiarly part of English history. Its founders had been important in the Old World, and in coming to the New they intended to *influence* English society, not escape from it. There were always figures in English public life—Cromwell, Algernon Sidney, Bolingbroke, and John Wilkes, for example—with whom New Englanders could identify and whom they could suppose would 're-direct' England on paths entirely congenial to the men of Massachusetts. Even Jonathan Mayhew's famous sermon on 'Unlimited Submission' in 1750, which Adams said made a 'great sensation' and was 'a tolerable catechism' for future revolutionists, was re-published in England and denounced a tyranny as *potentially* reprehensible in Old England as in New.

At Harvard College Adams studied mathematics and natural philosophy under John Winthrop, a member of the Royal Society. After his graduation, as a teacher and apprentice lawyer in Worcester, he read and talked at length about religion, history, and government—all in an English context. Then, as Boston rejoiced over the British conquest of Canada, Adams heard James Otis' stirring protest that Writs of Assistance were 'against the fundamental principles of laws'; that is, they violated a higher, natural law than those decreed in London and thus could have no legitimate authority. Adams left the courtroom deeply impressed, 'ready to take up arms against writs of assistance'. He also later recalled that 'the Child Independence was born' at the moment of Otis' speech.[11] His old age recollections doubtless exaggerated both the effect of Otis' speech on him and its influence in stimulating colonial resistance to the mother country, but a fateful issue had been raised—and there could be no doubt of Adams' choice should he find *British* law contrary to *natural* law.

In 1765 he wrote a 'Dissertation on the Canon and Feudal Law' (as it was titled when reprinted in England) denouncing 'a direct and formal design a foot to enslave all America'. He invoked British tradition to resist the schemes of the Grenville ministry: 'Let us take it for granted', he wrote, 'that the same spirit which once gave Caesar such a warm welcome, which [announced] hostilities against John till Magna Charta was signed, which severed the head of Charles the First from his body and drove James the Second from his kingdom...is still alive and active and warm in England.' In asking that 'every sluice of knowledge be opened and set flowing' to form a torrent of opposition to the iniquitous Stamp Act, Adams called upon British Whig spokesmen: 'The Brookses, Hampdens, Vanes, Seldens, Miltons, Nedhams, Harringtons, Nevilles, Sidneys, and Lockes'. Proud of the words and deeds of resistance to tyranny throughout the colonies, Adams wrote of 1765 as a momentous year—and it was as well a year he would have scarcely believed possible in 1755.[12] He had held the acts of his British rulers up against hallowed principles and put principles *first* in his allegiance. He still hoped the rulers would return to the principles, but he knew ultimately where he would stand.

Through the tumultuous decade 1765–75, events, harangues, and disquisitions combined to corrode John and Abigail Adams' sense of Englishness, to nourish their sense of distinctive

Americanness, and to make them ready for the events of July 1776. As Congress adopted the Declaration of Independence, John, looking 'back to the Year 1761', was 'surprised at the Suddenness, as well as Greatness of this Revolution'. It was the will of Heaven, it seemed, 'that the two Countries should be sundered forever'. He and his wife were now prepared to accept that. Though 'well aware of the Toil and Blood and Treasure that it will cost us to maintain this Declaration', John saw 'Rays of ravishing light and Glory...[wherein] Posterity will try-umph'.[13] He could now consign himself and his family to the destiny of being *American*; he had a new loyalty.

John Adams discovered the complexity of his Anglo-American identity, though, on his diplomatic missions to the Continent. Upon landing in Bordeaux in 1778, 'the fields of Grain, the Vineyards, the Castles, the Cities, the Parks, [and] the Gardens' utterly charmed him, but he was appalled at the 'swarms of beggars' on the streets, uncared for, he observed, in contrast to the poor in England and America attended to by the parish authorities. At a welcoming dinner, he nearly swallowed his spoon when an elegant French lady, noting that his name was *Adams*, asked if his family knew how the first man and woman 'found out the art of lying together'. He confided in his diary that 'if such are the manners of Women of Rank, Fashion and Reputation in France, they can never support a Republi-can Government...We must therefore take great care not to import them into America.' In a journey across Spain he found the roads abominable and the condition of the populace wretched: 'I see nothing but Signs of Poverty and Misery among the People. A fertile Country not half cultivated, People ragged and dirty, and the Houses universally nothing but Mire, Smoke, Fleas, and Lice. Nothing appears rich but the Church, nobody fat, but the Clergy.'[14]

When Adams reached London in 1785 to take up his post as first American Minister to Britain, he was in some ways more at home, but the lack of egalitarian simplicity that had troubled Franklin soon grieved Adams as well. Upon reflection, and thinking of the contrast between New England and the more aristocratic American South as well, he concluded that four institutions in New England, the town meeting, the local militia, the primary school, and the congregational church made 'Knowledge and Dexterity at Public Business common, [assured] a frequent Division of landed Property [that] prevents Monopolies of Land,...and supported Religion, Morals, and Decency'.[15] He had in fact identified a social system moulding the everyday life of the community that was the flesh and blood of the skeletal 'self-government' provided for in the new constitutions. The purpose and character of the new nation, the focus of Adams' loyalty if you like, was, like Franklin's, a way of life for the common people. For the first thirty or forty years of his life he saw no contradiction between this way and a British nationality; indeed, the enterprising, bourgeois, Puritan England of his mind's eye was its source. What he had seen between 1765 and 1775 was a pattern of events posing a grave threat to the institutions and values which in Massachusetts underlay community life. If soldiers could be quartered, what then of the militia? If a bishop could be appointed, what then of congregationalism? If a charter could be abrogated, what then of local self-rule? Society itself would soon be grievously changed.

If this is a fair picture of Adams' revolutionary loyalties, many puzzling aspects of his later thought and career become more explicable. His conservatism embodied reverence for a long tradition of habits of life in old and New England, a conviction that forms and symbols were important in a nation's life, a strong sense of law and order, and a perception that the modes of government in the new United States were peculiar to itself. Thus he had only scorn and contempt for theorists such as Paine and Condorcet who sought either to apply Anglo-American conceptions of self-government in France or Russia or whatever, or to reduce government by consent to a representative, unitary assembly acting according to majority vote. Thus he sought state support for Harvard College and the Congregational Church as valuable institutions supporting public enlightenment and morality. Thus as well, though, he hated in the depth of his being Hamilton's notion of a fast-and-loose, expansionist super-state likely to ride recklessly over towns like Braintree, Massachusetts.

To put it another way, Adams took the social fabric very seriously indeed. This of course put him closer to Loyalists like

Joseph Galloway and Jonathan Boucher than to revolutionists like Paine or many of the Pennsylvania constitutionalists of 1776—or to Alexander Hamilton. The key difference between Adams and most Loyalists, though, was his conception of what sort of society should be preserved and how far one should go in formal obedience and allegiance in order to avoid the admitted perils of social disruption. Adams' society of town, school, church, and militia was quite different from Boucher's of parish, bishop, gentry, and crown, just as his Puritan idea that one's deepest allegiance was to a way sanctioned in higher law was poles apart from Boucher's insistence upon final obedience to the reigning monarch. John and Abigail Adams were resolute in coming to their revolutionary disavowal of loyalty because they had within them, perhaps unarticulated in 1776, firm notions of what the purpose of a new nation should be and what habits, values, and institutions needed to be encouraged to give it an admired character and way of life.

IV

Thomas Jefferson shared Adams' deep appreciation of English culture and his complex sense of social order. Jefferson read as earnestly as Adams in English law and history, and when in 1774 he invoked the usages of Saxon England and of the foes of Charles I and James II against George III, he thought he spoke as a liberty-loving Englishman ought to speak. Yet, as younger and more speculative than Franklin and Adams, and never linked by rumour as they were with loyalism, Jefferson came with less difficulty to think in the universal, natural-rights terms of the Declaration of Independence. But he soon turned to the details: after July 1776 he went home to Virginia to remould her laws and local institutions according to the new republican model. Like Franklin and Adams, he believed a rejected national loyalty, and even formal statements and frames of government, were the beginning, not the fulfilment of new nationhood.

Jefferson turned first to the land system, of prime importance, of course, to one of his already pronounced physiocratic inclinations. The old system of primogeniture and entail, he wrote, entrenched a 'Patrician order, distinguished by [their] splendor and luxury' and by their monopoly of the government. He proposed instead a division of property 'to make an opening for the aristocracy of virtue and talent, which nature had wisely provided for the direction of society, and scattered with equal hand through all its conditions'. Such a scheme, he insisted, 'was essential to a well-ordered republic'. Next, the state needed to provide free primary education for all children so they 'would be qualified to understand their rights, to maintain them and to exercise with intelligence, their parts in self-government'.[16] He also urged reform of the courts and other agencies of local government to give the people a maximum sense of participation and responsiveness.

He attended carefully to these details because, like his Loyalist opponents, he regarded government by the people as fraught with danger. To prevent abuses it was necessary to cultivate a proper social order, and good sense in the people, the individual citizens, who were to govern. First, he theorized, the citizen needed an occupation that would develop the skills of citizenship: self-reliance, industry, and attachment to the community; obviously farming was the answer. To further encourage this occupation, and to give men a stake in society as eighteenth-century political thinking generally required, Jefferson proposed that the state give 50 or 100 acres of land to each of its landless citizens—then a freehold requirement for voting would be inclusive rather than exclusive. The pyramided education system, providing rudiments for ordinary citizens and advanced learning to those whose talents marked them as leaders, would properly diffuse the skills without which, Jefferson had no doubt, self-government would be as bad as a government by a stupid or evil king or aristocracy. With proper training thus provided, he insisted on constant practice in self-government at the local level to equip citizens to make the judgments required in state and national government. Freedom of religion, freedom of expression, and procedural due process were also critical devices for insuring the exchange of ideas and the freedom from intimidation vital to meaningful self-government. Jeffersons's loyalty, then, enlarged and made more sophisticated by the opportunities of Independence, came, like Franklin's and

Adams's, to encompass a comprehensive social philosophy seeking to nourish and guide the people in manifold ways. He was as much concerned about personal habits and values as Poor Richard and as much concerned about social institutions as the selectman of Braintree, Massachusetts. He sought in Virginia after 1776 to begin the task of reforming everyday life on a republican model that would, in time, embody the national character.

Even Jefferson's views on slavery, incidentally, fit this general outlook. Being convinced, as were nearly all Europeans in the eighteenth century, that blacks were inherently inferior to whites, but nonetheless human beings, clearly he had to make special provisions for them. If they were unequal, they could not be awarded the same privileges and responsibilities as whites without creating an endless, invidious, unfair divisiveness in society. The existing system resting on the supposed inequality, however, slavery, was abhorrent to Jerfferson's sense of justice, human dignity, and republicanism. He agreed with Franklin that the status of both degraded slave and arrogant master poisoned the personal qualities vital to a self-governing society. Jefferson therefore proposed the gradual abolition of slavery to be accompanied by the resettlement of the freed blacks in the American west. There, free from what he believed was the inevitable discrimination by 'superior' white people, they could develop their own peculiar kind of society, and white society would itself be able to grow in an entirely republican way, unfettered by the curse of slavery and the moral compromises implicit in a community of unequal persons. The flaw in Jefferson's outlook was not in the proposals he made for adjusting republican forms to an assumed inferiority, but, of course, the assumption in the first place.

As with Franklin and Adams, Jefferson's years in Europe as an American diplomat sharpened his sense of the essential qualities of life in the new nation. Travels in the French countryside always heightened his conviction that landless peasants could never be a foundation for republican government. More personally, as he considered his daughter's education and that of nephews who wanted to come to Europe to study, he came to agree with Franklin's judgment (and sad experience with his son and grandsons) that a European education unsuited one for life in the New World.

> Let us view [he wrote] the disadvantages of sending a youth to Europe [for his education]...If he goes to England he learns drinking, horse-racing, and boxing...He acquires [anywhere] a fondness for European luxury and dissipation, and a contempt for the simplicity of his own country; he is fascinated with the privileges of the European aristocrats, and...contracts a partiality for [them]. He is led, by the strongest of all human passions, into a spirit for female intrigue, destructive of his own and others' happiness, or a passion for whores, destructive of his health;...he recollects the voluptuary dress and arts of the European women, and pities and despises the chaste affections and simplicity of those of his own country;...he returns to his own country, a foreigner, unacquainted with the practices of domestic economy necessary to preserve him from ruin... It appears to me, then, that an American, coming to Europe for an education, loses in his knowledge, in his morals, in his health, in his habits, and in his happiness.[17]

If this seems puritanical and provincial even for someone as straight-laced as Jefferson usually was, we should remember that he wrote it at a time when the European experience had excited him to intense, creative thinking about his own loyalty and identity. He, like Franklin, loved the sophisticated, elegant life of Paris. Among other things, he acquired a taste for fine wine that, together with his Virginian generosity, kept him in debt for the rest of his life! Yet, thinking of the inequities upon which that elegance rested, and the on-going requirements of family and community life, he overwhelmingly favoured the New World pattern. He saw more clearly, too, how his republican social philosophy was inconsistent with the customs and paraphernalia of government in the Old World. Every little detail seemed important. Not only were titles and deferential forms of address anathema, but when he became president Jefferson deliberately undertook to 'republicanize' what he and his followers ridiculed as 'The Federalist Court'. He abolished precedent at the White House dinner table in a way that created an international incident, and he received foreign ministers in slippers not because he was careless about his dress, or forgot, but because it suited his sense of republican simplicity. He not only scorned the forms but sought to undo the very notion that government was something grand and above and separate from the people. He enshrined Bacon, Newton, and Locke as his 'trinity of immortals', not Julius Caesar whom Hamilton preferred, and he sought remembrance for the Declaration of Independence, the Virginia statute for religious freedom, and the founding of the University of Virginia, rather than for any of the great offices of state he had held—and he never had any title except that of Mr Jefferson in an age when men of distinction commonly sought to be Colonel or General or Lord or whatever. In his four careers as revolutionist, as diplomat, as political leader, and as sage he set before his countrymen a conception of nationhood full and compelling enough to call forth over and over again in American history invocations of his name—to be 'Jeffersonian', whatever the perversions of that designation, has had meaning down to the present moment. Consider Adlai Stevenson and Eugene McCarthy for examples. Stevenson's lucid rhetoric, his sense of justice, his humaneness, and his international idealism are all Jeffersonian echoes, while McCarthy's disgust at a military-complex run amuck and his pledge to diminish the office of the presidency rest upon a Jeffersonian suspicion of an aggrandizing (Hamiltonian) government grown too large and too remote from the people. Jefferson's ultimate national loyalty, we might say, then, was to a social system and mode of government only hinted at in the Declaration of Independence. His enduring appeal measures the richness of his mature conception.

V

I hope these three patterns reveal that, for men of deep cultural understanding and intellectual inclination at least, a change of national loyalty involved much more than a formal shift of allegiance. They sensed very well that to disavow loyalty substantially diminished them—they had to contemplate being without affections, associations, and satisfactions enjoyed and cherished since birth. They had to face as well years of struggle, and turmoil, and danger that, except for the most alienated and restless individuals, seemed more likely to disturb and uproot than to nourish and sustain. This sense of cultural loss and abhorrence of social disorder meant, of course, that men like Franklin and Adams had a substantial common understanding with men like Galloway and Boucher. Why, then, did some opt for Independence?

Most basically, it seems to me, the signers of the Declaration of Independence had a view of life and a commitment to values that, as they thought excruciatingly about it in the years before 1776, seemed viable without a formal British loyalty, and, in fact, might be gravely threatened by that loyalty. Loyalists puzzled over the same question but could not, ultimately, see themselves meaningfully without a British nationality. This could be because they had a very deep sense of cultural continuity, such, for example, as that of Provost William Smith of the College of Philadelphia. Others, like Jonathan Boucher, so emphasized the need for obedience and social order that they could not countenance revolution on any grounds at all. Still others, like Governor Thomas Hutchinson of Massachusetts, though of impeccable New England background, frankly admired a hierarchical social system and an imperial frame of government that could only be sustained, he believed, within the British Empire. In any case they did not conceive a society wherein they could lead lives of promise and dignity apart from the mother country. They were thus unable to consummate the revolution John Adams said was over by 1776.

The revolutionists, on the other hand, in the final analysis gave their allegiance to a society with a texture of everyday life ultimately transcending flags, oaths to the crown, and even birthright. Franklin, Adams, and Jefferson each characteristically revealed the life style to which he assigned prime allegiance. Franklin's *Autobiography*, though its first and most significant part was written in 1771 at the country home of an Anglican bishop when he was feeling very comfortable with his Englishness, displays dramatically the New World way of life, possible, of course, in Britain, but as he came increasingly to see, not likely to be dominant in the England of George III. John Adams grew up in an environment of classic appeal: the New England town of self-governing yeoman farmers. As an Empire enthusiast in 1758, as a revolutionist in 1776, as a traveller in

Europe in 1780, as a conservative theorist of government in 1787, as a Franco-phobe president in 1798, and as a friend of Jefferson's in the 1820s, Adams' goal remained the same: to build and sustain a society that would embody the virtues of the New England town. Jefferson's genius, and compelling vision, was to fashion the social philosophy and the political practices that would give substance to the rather abstract republicanism of the Declaration of Independence. His boundless curiosity and concern for every detail of human society originated in his conviction that the daily life of the citizens of a republic had to embody the qualities essential to the working of that form of government: self-reliance, good judgment, community responsibility, and a degree of optimism about the future of the human race. Each man, that is, came to realize, first that for him a way of life transcended his national loyalty, then that a new form and purpose of government had to be declared and devised, and finally that a complex pattern of attitudes, values, habits, and institutions would have to mature before the new nation achieved a character and a self-respect in the world. This large conception, and the persistent, creative effort to bring it closer to realization, were the most profoundly revolutionary qualities of Franklin, Adams, and Jefferson, and the features that most fundamentally distinguished them from those who remained loyal to Britain.

NOTES

All quotations are from the standard printed works of Franklin, Adams, or Jefferson.

1. Rush to Price, 25 May 1786, L. H. Butterfield (ed.), *The Letters of Benjamin Rush*, 2 vols, Princeton, N.J., 1951, I, 388-9.

2. Franklin, 'Observations Concerning the Increase of Mankind', L. W. Labaree and others (eds.), *The Papers of Benjamin Franklin*, New Haven, Conn., IV, 227-34.

3. Ibid.

4. Article signed 'Pensylvanus', *Penna. Journal* supplement, 25 March 1956.

5. To William Franklin, 19 February 1772 and to Mary Stevenson, 25 March 1763, A. H. Smyth (ed.), *The Writings of Benjamin Franklin*, 10 vols, N.Y., 1905-7, V, 414; IV, 194.

6. To Joseph Galloway, 17 February 1758 and 12 April 1766, R. L. Ketcham (ed.), *The Political Thought of Benjamin Franklin*, Indianapolis, 1965, pp. 144-5; to Isaac Norris, 10 March 1757 and Thomas Penn to Richard Peters, 14 May 1757, *Papers of Franklin*, VIII, 291-7, VII, 110-11n.

7. To Joshua Babcock, 13 January 1772, *Pol. Thought of Franklin*, pp. 244–5.

8. *A History of the English Speaking Peoples: The Age of Revolution*, N.Y., 1957, p. 182.

9. To Sarah Bache, 1 January 1784, *Writings of Franklin*, IX, 161–7.

10. Ibid., VIII, 603–14.

11. L. H. Butterfield and others (eds.), *The Diary and Autobiography of John Adams*, 4 vols, Cambridge, Mass., 1961, III, 262–75.

12. G. A. Peek (ed.), *The Political Writings of John Adams*, Indianapolis, 1954, pp. 18–21.

13. John to Abigail Adams, 3 July 1776, L. H. Butterfield and others (eds.), *Adams Family Correspondence*, Cambridge, Mass., 1963, II, 28–31.

14. 26 April 1778, 27 December 1779 and 5 February 1780, *Diary of Adams*, IV, 35–40; II, 415–34.

15. 16 and 21 July 1786, ibid., III, 194–5.

16. A. Koch and W. Peden (eds.), *The Life and Selected Writings of Thomas Jefferson*, N.Y., 1944, pp. 265–6, from 'Notes on Virginia', written in 1782.

17. Jefferson to J. Banister, 15 October 1785, ibid., pp. 386–7.

The Aftermath of Revolution

The Loyalists and British Policy[1]

CHARLES RITCHESON

At the end of the war for Independence, American hatred for the 'tories', traitors within the gates, exceeded the feeling against even the British. Henry Laurens, but recently out of the Tower of London in 1782, expressed the general attitude. 'How are the Refugees to be provided for? They are yours,' he told British questioners; 'maintain them—had they honestly remain'd with us, they would not have been Beggars.' Harsh, but worse was to come as he warmed to his theme. 'With what face can any Man say either by himself or his Council [*sic*] to Congress, "I am a Loyalist, I used my utmost Endeavors to get you all hanged and to confiscate your Estates and beggar your Wives and Children: Pray make a Provision for me or let me enjoy my Estate".' The British principle of war had been 'to pay the Charges out of forfeited Estates, deducting the Expence of Halters'. The Tories had acted in aid of that principle. Now, let them suffer.[2]

The passions of war are never pretty and rarely lend themselves to the making of fine distinctions. Laurens' terrible anger took no account of the thousands of decent, honourable, and conscientious men whose sense of duty, deeply and honestly held, required them to support the old order. Some Americans were more moderate than the outranged and irascible Laurens, but for the first few years of restored peace the issue remained a highly emotional one, charged with great bitterness and wounded sensibilities on both sides of the Atlantic.[3]

British and American negotiators in Paris in 1782, after very hard bargaining, finally wrote into the peace preliminaries two articles dealing with Loyalists. One (Article V) promised that Congress would 'earnestly recommend' to the individual states the restoration of property and rights confiscated from 'real British subjects' during the war. The same benefit would be extended to residents in areas held by British forces, if they had not borne arms against the United States. For a year, Loyalists would be permitted free entry and peaceable residence within the territories of the United States while they sought restitution of their losses. (Wartime purchasers of Loyalist property would be entitled to a return of their money.) Congress would also recommend a 'reconsideration and revision' of all laws touching the Loyalists passed by the states. The object would be to render these laws consistent with justice, equity, and conciliation. Returning refugees would not meet with legal impediment in the pursuit of their rights.

The second article (Article VI) provided an amnesty; forbade further confiscations, persecutions, or arrests; and promised the cessation of prosecutions in progress. It should be noted that the 'recommend' provision in Article V, so important a feature of the future American defence against British charges of treaty-breaking, made no part of Article VI. The preliminary treaty was signed on 30 November 1782, and subsequently became definitive on 3 September 1783.

The Loyalist provisions were certainly minimal in view of the exiles' contributions to the royal cause and the sufferings these entailed; and they were seized upon by Shelburne's enemies in Parliament to help in overturning the ministry. North's friends, out of office since the end of the war, were especially violent. Alexander Wedderburn, Lord Loughborough, for example, even on his honeymoon found his 'repose' destroyed by news of the unsatisfactory terms for the Loyalists. The old ministry to which he had belonged had seen losses, to be sure, he fulminated to his friend William Eden; but they were 'only such as the fortune of war may produce in spite of Valor or of Wisdom'. (Apparently he had forgotten his recent savage criticisms of Lords North and George Germain.) 'But', he continued, striking a rare note of righteous indignation, 'to make a gratuitous sacrifice of the rights of the State and of the national faith, to proclaim ourselves beaten Cowards incapable of protecting the Adherents to our wretched fortune, is such a Loss of Credit as no Calamity of War should have made a People submit to.'[4] Lord

North, his own distaste for politics overcome by a period in the wilderness, summoned his followers to the opening of the parliamentary session to do battle against 'this base Treatment of the Loyalists'.[5] Despite the unconscious irony in their hot espousal of the Loyalists' cause—no one had done more to bring the refugees to their sorry state than those who had mismanaged the American War—the issue was critical, indeed fatal, for the Shelburne ministry. The Earl's own apologia—that a part would have to suffer to prevent the destruction of the whole—was scarcely designed to rally the nation to his side; and the hapless First Minister departed with the triumph of his enemies and the maledictions of the Loyalists ringing in his ears. For his successors, the coalition ministry, there was reserved the cold comfort of accepting the provisional treaty unchanged as the definitive settlement.

That the Loyalist issue played a major part in overthrowing Shelburne is clear. But what of the assertion, frequently made, that after the war the exiles exercised an important, even determining influence in the formulation of British policy towards the United States? John Adams, minister plenipotentiary in London, for example, faced with the ruin of his British diplomacy, attributed much of his failure to the refugees. Even Shelburne, not to mention the coalition and Pitt ministries, he believed to possess an 'immoderate attachment' for the exiles. Venomous and vengeful, the Tories, he thought, were scheming to persuade the British government to a 'new system': fortification of the Canadian border, construction of a Great Lakes fleet, intrigue among the Indians, and the retention of the posts in the Old Northwest ceded to the Republic by the treaty of peace.

Adams' convictions and suspicions were shared by many of his fellow citizens, among them Thomas Jefferson and John Jay. As late as 1790, Gouverneur Morris, President Washington's unofficial envoy to London, accounted for his own diplomatic fiasco by blaming the Tory exiles, motivated, he said, by the desire to recoup wartime 'losses and disappointments'.[6]

The West Indians echoed and reinforced the charges, holding Loyalist plotters responsible for the defeat of their favourite design, winning admission for American vessels into their ports.

Bryan Edwards saw in the Committee for Trade's Report of 31 May 1784 the imprint of the refugees—men, he declared, who possessed 'a lurking taint of resentment and malignity' and a desire 'to wound the new republic through the sides of the West Indies'.[7]

In the face of a multitude of statements like these, even the mildest scepticism might appear to rest on mere crankiness. Unanimity generates its own doubt, however; and a certain suspicion attaches to the vague and insubstantial evidence commonly adduced by those who assert that Loyalists exercised an important and formative influence in determining Britain's post-war policy towards the United States.

If the allegations are true, a number of exceedingly important analytical questions require answers; yet none has ever been forthcoming, at least to my satisfaction. How was Loyalist influence exerted? Was it wielded by a numerous, well-organized, and effectively-led 'lobby'? Or was it the result of secret machinations by a few forceful individuals who operated behind the curtains? What were specific instances of successful Loyalist manipulation of British policy? If we adopt the 'lobby' theory, then a fundamental problem is that of number, particularly, of refugees who would certainly be the active agents. (Erstwhile Loyalists who did *not* migrate would scarcely draw further jeopardy upon themselves by plots and intrigues against the victors.)

The truth is that data presently available about number are hopelessly incomplete. There are statements which sound authoritative—like John Adams' famous division of the American population into thirds—but which are at best very rough approximations or even literary conceits. Professor William H. Nelson has given us a useful and illuminating study in his *The American Tory*; but he gives even less satisfaction than Adams when he states that Loyalists constituted one-third and Revolutionists two-thirds of the 'politically active population'. Wallace Brown's *The King's Friends* is even more disappointing, perhaps because it promises so much. Basing himself chiefly on Benjamin F. Stevens' transcripts taken in 1900 from the claims commission records, he conjectures that 'most men of "parts" were Patriots'. One observation bears, correctly, I think, but obliquely on the question of Loyalist influence. Tory leadership, Brown writes, 'could not remotely match the Whigs in talents'.

Rightly critical of R. R. Palmer's unsupported assertion that there were 24 Loyalist exiles per 1000 population (compared with 5 per 1000 in the French Revolution), and of Evart B. Greene's and John R. Alden's estimates, Brown prefers Phineas Bond's contemporary guess of 100 000, although he believes the total might well have been as low as 80 000. By a complicated line of reasoning—he has to assume that each active Loyalist who went into exile took with him a family of 5 or 6—Brown produces a total of 160 000 to 192 000 who left the United States. He concludes rather lamely, however, 'that no accurate count can ever be made, and it may well be that the precise number is comparatively unimportant'.[8]

The number who bore arms for the King is an easier problem; and Paul H. Smith appears to have solved it as well as evidence now available allows in his excellent article 'The American Loyalists: Notes on their Organization and Numerical Strength', published in 1968 in the *William and Mary Quarterly*.[9] Even here, the margin of error is admittedly large, however. As for those who stood silent, choosing to submit to a new order they detested or accepted reluctantly, their number can never be even reasonably approximated.

In short, there has been a great deal of wheel-spinning on the subject of Loyalists' numbers. Bond's estimate seems sounder than most, and he is at least a contemporary source. As for secondary sources, the estimates made by Fiske in 1888 and Bradley in 1932, that is, from 60 000 to 100 000 are close to Bond's estimate; and taken together, they furnish a reasonable working hypothesis which subsequent works have not superseded.[10] Of these, it may be assumed that about one-half, including many former slaves, settled in Nova Scotia and in what would presently become New Brunswick. Another 10 000 supplied the flesh and bone for Governor Simcoe's Upper Canada. Several thousand, also including many slaves, found new homes in the British West Indies. But by far the largest portion of this second half went to the British Isles. Whatever the precise number, then, it is obvious from the outset that the Loyalists, scattered as they were, did not constitute a single, united body lobbying on questions of policy at White-hall.

The many thousands who settled in England were danger-ously close to the centre of power, however. Did they, perhaps, constitute a 'lobby' aspiring to seize the ministerial tiller on American questions? Certainly, many among them returned Henry Laurens' terrible hatred in full measure. As they sought to adapt themselves to new and straitened circumstances, their daily lives were abiding reminders of past misfortunes and their causes. Given the opportunity, they would surely exercise any available influence to persuade British policy makers to take a hard line toward the United States. Again, geography worked against them. Scattered throughout the kingdom, Loyalist exiles never achieved the unity of purpose or even of spirit which might have made them formidable in the eyes of government. Various committees emerged; but the evidence shows their pre-occupation to have been the pursuit of pensions and com-pensation for war-time losses.

Further, the Loyalist émigrés to Britain were an exceedingly heterogeneous lot. Some had borne arms for the King, and had lost their all. Others had been merchants or agents only tem-porarily resident in the colonies. Numerous young professional men like the lawyer George Chalmers had similarly gone out to America for a relatively brief residence to gain experience and perhaps a stake before returning to Britain. Former members of the colonial 'establishment' were represented in considerable number. Most tenuously connected of all were absentee land-lords—John Knox, for example, who lost property through war-time confiscations. In short, it is clear that Loyalists in Britain possessed no single and unifying set of interests; and in at least one important instance, there was indeed a major, even violent conflict within their ranks. British merchants expelled during the war wanted desperately to retrieve their pre-war debts in America and were far more interested in cultivating good relations with the United States than in supporting anti-American lucubrations.[11] Doubtless many other Loyalists also hoped to reach private settlement of their affairs in America, and would thus favour the restoration of a friendly intercourse with the erstwhile rebels.

If we discard the idea of a numerous and unified Loyalist 'lobby', what then of the suggestion that a small number of talented, influential, and well-placed men worked behind the scenes to influence Britain's American policy? A considerable number were certainly experienced in the ways of political life and in the exercise of power—former governors, magistrates, customs officers, members of colonial assemblies, and the like.[12] Among these, Thomas Hutchinson, formerly governor of Massachusetts, was the most illustrious. Received at court and made something of a celebrity upon arrival, he might well have been influential in ministerial circles (although he himself doubted it); but he died in 1780. John Tabor Kempe, late attorney-general of New York; William Smith, chief justice of the same province; Harrison Gray of Boston; and Joseph Galloway of Pennsylvania were all prominent members of the former colonial 'establishment'. Doubtless there were attempts to gain the ear of the powerful; but ministerial doors did not open easily. Joseph Galloway, for example, holding no official position, tried very hard to establish himself as the government's resident expert on American affairs. Long, rambling, and finally bitter letters were addressed to the Earl of Hardwicke, the only friend he had who could pretend to an entrée among the political mighty. The noble lord's pipeline to the higher reaches of government was limited, perhaps by design, to Under-secretary of State George Aust, who read the letters passed on to him by Hardwicke and forgot them.[13] Thomas Hutchinson, shortly before his death, summed up the plight of Loyalists like himself. 'We Americans are plenty here, and very cheap', he wrote. 'Some of us at first coming, are apt to think ourselves of importance, but other people do not think so, and few, if any of us are much consulted, or enquired after.'[14]

Hutchinson was speaking for his own generation, of course, men who passed rather quickly from the scene. There remained younger men of talent, less well-known, perhaps, but more vigorous and active. Did they take the lead in efforts to influence policy on behalf of the Loyalists? George Chalmers, erstwhile resident of Maryland, won the notice and respect of Charles Jenkinson, who in 1786 made him First Clerk of the reorganized Committee for Trade and Plantations. The late Professor Harlow has called him Jenkinson's right-hand man and a principal agent in the execution of British policy towards the United States;[15] but it is perfectly clear from a study of Jenkinson's voluminous papers that whatever influence Chalmers enjoyed he derived from his role as a devoted and hard-working assistant, not as an *éminence grise*. In any event, by the time of Chalmers' appointment in 1786, the fundamentals of British policy towards America had already been laid down. Brook Watson, wartime commissary-general of the troops in North America, and William Knox, who never forgot nor forgave the loss of his property in Georgia, were Members of Parliament and active in subministerial levels of government. Knox claimed chief responsibility for the Order in Council of 2 July 1783, which shut British West Indian ports to American vessels; but the evidence shows that his real function was essentially that of the clerk—to incorporate in written form decisions already made by his superiors. Whatever the case, to call Knox or Watson 'loyalist sufferers', as Professor Helen Taft Manning has done,[16] is surely to stretch the meaning of the term to the breaking point. William Smith wielded considerable influence as a trusted adviser of Sir Guy Carleton, who went out as Lord Dorchester to govern Canada. He was scarcely the vengeful ogre John Adams suspected him to have been, however, since it was with Smith's advice that Dorchester opened the overland trade routes with the United States. Lieutenant-General John Simcoe, an energetic, feared, and effective adversary in war, became governor of the new province of Upper Canada when it was created in 1791. The outbreak of war in Europe and the mutual suspicion of Canadians (among them many refugees) and Americans very nearly brought an extension of hostilities to the New World; and Simcoe's military initiative along the frontier must be reckoned an important element in the near collision. The thrill of the near miss often obscures the fundamental fact that peace in the backcountry *was* preserved between Britain and America by men more powerful than Simcoe. Nor could the general's greatest exertions persuade the British government to treat with a virtually independent Vermont at a time when it appeared altogether possible that the province might be induced to return to its allegiance to the crown.

Finally, even Simcoe himself looked forward to some future Anglo-American family compact.[17]

Other Loyalists found places in the new British consular service in the United States. Sir John Temple, self-styled baronet, became first consul-general at New York. Related distantly by blood to the Marquis of Buckingham and by marriage to Governor Bowdoin of Massachusetts, he devoted what zeal he possessed to making the best of both worlds. Pompous, vain, and petty-minded, Temple sent home dispatches which were superficial, hopelessly incomplete, and generally incompetent. They influenced his government to a certain degree, to be sure: Phineas Bond, himself a Loyalist, was sent out to be consul, and later consul-general for the Middle States, thereby limiting severely Temple's area of responsibility. By contrast, Bond was the perfect consular official. Prompt and painstaking in executing orders from home, he was indefatigable in collecting and reporting mercantile data; and he was ever on guard to protect British commercial and maritime interests within his province. Esteemed and respected by his superiors, Bond supplied much valuable information to the home authorities; but the formulation of policy he left to others. At one point, he sought urgently even frantically to persuade the ministry to exclude American vessels from Britain's Far Eastern trading preserves, but he was ignored; and his most eloquent arguments against admitting American vessels of limited tonnage into British West Indian ports in 1794 were to no avail.

Colonel John Hamilton became consul in Virginia and George Miller in South Carolina and Georgia. Both acquitted themselves well in the discharge of their duties, but they, like Bond, were the gatherers of data, not the fashioners of policy. The list of Loyalists in relatively minor office could doubtless be extended, but a single observation applies to them all: they adapted to the system, choosing to make new careers, not to pursue old vendettas. They became the tools of policy, not the makers of it; while the great majority of their fellows, preoccupied with their own self-interests, lacked even this limited influence.

Politically innocuous they may have been; but they did

command public sympathy and compassion, at least for a time. Soon after the war, the *Morning Herald* and the *Morning Chronicle* indignantly likened the exiles to the royalists who had fled the tyranny of Cromwell. 'Persecuted without intermission', one of them raged, 'by a cruel, relentless, bigotted, consequential, in their own opinions, deluded and infatuate race of men,' they and their posterity would 'remember to the latest ages, the unjust and inhuman acts of the lawless banditti'.[18] Sympathy took the form, too, of hard cash. With no material assistance to be expected from the United States, the British government undertook the expensive task of compensating the sufferers and affording them a measure of financial relief. Individual grants were not large—George Chalmers, for example, was given a pension of £100 a year—but by 1782, something in excess of £40 000 was being paid out each year, and in addition there were exceptional grants totalling £17 000–£18 000 a year. With peace established, expenditure rose enormously. Under an act of Parliament passed in the summer of 1783, a commission was created to investigate and validate Loyalist claims; and in 1785 the Chairman, John Anstey, and two fellow commissioners went out to the New World to collect information on the spot. Even before the commission reported, the government paid out about £3 million to Loyalists. The refugees in Canada also received about £2 million, including the cost of provisions (for two years), tools, lumber, surveying fees, and other similar items. In 1788, an additional £1⅓ million was paid out; and by 1789 pensions were amounting to more than £1 million. By that time, the Loyalists had cost Britain about £7 500 000, roughly twice the interest on the national debt in 1763.[19] Loyalist pensions continued beyond 1789, of course. The total outlay would thus continue to grow. This was a gauge of British sympathy, and gratitude, however, not of Loyalist influence in the formation of grant policy. Presently, even sympathy and gratitude began to wane.

Loyalists who elected to make new homes in the remaining colonies—rebuilding the strength of the shattered empire—rarely found the mother country flagging in her support. The Committee for Trade's Report of 31 May 1784 stated that one (though by no means the only) reason for discriminating against

American vessels in the West Indies was the desire to open for the overseas Loyalists an opportunity to move into the maritime vacuum created by the secession of the former colonies. The refugees at 'home' in Britain, however, were another matter. Many became disillusioned with life about them, indulging in impossible dreams of returning to the native land and drawing together in their clubs and committees, a group apart, ever more isolated from the mainstream of British life. In pursuit of pensions and compensations, some proved grasping and mendacious, thus giving a bad name to all. Within a year of the peace, there were signs that some Britons had come to begrudge charity itself; and while the desire to forget the unpleasant past was natural, the speed with which the refugees in the mother country found sympathy turning to disregard and even open disdain can only be termed callous. If ever there had been an opportunity for a Loyalist 'lobby' to take a hand in the formulation of Britain's American policy, it disappeared very quickly.

Reaction began even while public declarations of support for the exiles were at their warmest. Unfortunate they were, blandly wrote 'Impartial Reason' in the *Morning Chronicle*;[20] but in every 'state commotion' a few must suffer, and in the present instance numbers had been greatly exaggerated. Charges of greed and self-serving, some emanating from high places, soon followed. During the evacuation of Charleston, General Leslie the British commander exclaimed in exasperation to his superior, Sir Guy Carleton, that although he had given a plentiful supply of provisions—sufficient for three to six months—to every Loyalist leaving the place, there were no 'bounds to the unreasonable demands of all sorts of People'.[21] Benjamin Vaughan, on the periphery of the peace negotiations in Paris in 1782, urged Shelburne—doubtless at the prompting of Franklin—to ignore 'the noisy clamors' of the refugees and to remember that he could '*judge* more truly than they can *relate*'. From New York, Maurice Morgann, Shelburne's confidential secretary (who was involved in his chief's ill-fated and ill-judged attempt to hasten Anglo-American reconciliation by a direct approach to Congress), warned that Loyalists were not to be trusted; their advice was based solely on self-interest. An

American visitor in London, admittedly not the most objective agent, informed Alexander Hamilton that 'the Loyalists here are a great burden to the Government, and they know not how to ascertain the real losses they have suffer'd, for the Estimates presented to the Commissioners are swell'd to a most enormous Sum'. The soul of moderation, John Jay considered the claims to 'afford conclusive evidence of their inattention to truth and common decency'.[22]

The charges receive authoritative support from the commissioners of Loyalist claims. In their first report, dated 10 August 1784, in which they dealt with claims of 2063 Loyalists for compensation amounting to about £7 050 000, Anstey and his colleagues bluntly stated that the figure was grossly inflated. In a subsequent report in 1790, the commissioners showed that 216 persons had claimed £306 000. After close examination of evidence, only £66 125 was allowed.[23] Exaggeration had clearly passed into attempted fraud; and there was fastened upon the Loyalists, no doubt unjustly in the majority of cases, a reputation for persistent, unscrupulous, and dishonest pursuit of private enrichment at the public charge.

A true measure of Loyalist influence in Britain was provided in 1787. In April, Earl Bathurst, whose career as Lord Chancellor during much of the American War cast no lustre on that high office, introduced a bill into the House of Lords. Entitled 'An Act for the better preventing vexatious Suits being brought for the Recovery of Debts contracted in America previous to the Treaty of Peace', it was seconded by the cantankerous and incorrigible Lord Chancellor Thurlow. An apprehensive John Adams, in London as his country's first diplomatic representative, attributed the manoeuvre to Benedict Arnold and told John Jay that it 'shows the spirit of the present ministry'.[24] He was wrong.

Aiming to protect Loyalist debtors from American creditors suing in British courts, the bill was an ill-conceived effort to retaliate for the multitude of state laws which screened Americans from their British creditors in manifest and flagrant violation of the Treaty of Peace. Certain vocal elements among the Loyalists gave their enthusiastic support. The result was an immediate and violent collision with the important and well-organized Committee of Merchants trading to North America, many of whom held large amounts in pre-war debts. In a resolution of 13 April 1787 the merchants declared to the ministry that the bill

has a very dangerous Tendency, that its principle is repugnant to the 4th Article of the Treaty of Peace...that it may in its Consequence operate to increase the Difficulty of recovering Debts due from America to this Country, and therefore calls for the immediate Exertions of the Committee to prevent its passing into a Law.[25]

It was a very effective quietus, and the proposed legislation was quickly withdrawn; but the affair sparked an ugly controversy in the press, casting in the process much light on the political impotence of the exiles in Britain.

Soon after the bill had been thrown out, a Loyalist signing himself 'Plain Truth' published a letter in the *Morning Chronicle*, bitterly castigating the merchants who had opposed it. They had, it was charged, procured assignments of debts due to American creditors by Loyalists, as payment of debts due to themselves by those same Americans. The merchants, 'actuated by a strange enthusiastick predilection for the Americans', found themselves swindled out of millions in goods by former rebels; and, 'Plain Truth' concluded, they aimed now to recoup their losses from the Loyalists.[26]

A week later, there came a savage rejoinder. How long would 'Plain Truth', and his brethren 'abuse the patience of the people of England?' How long would they 'violate decency, humanity and truth?' Would they not be content with 'daily vomiting forth...froth and venom against the Citizens of the United States' without continually libelling fellow subjects and 'even an higher character'—a reference to the King—who thought them 'a mischievous and troublesome set of people?' The merchants had not caused the war—a vicious thrust—but they bore the burden of it. Meantime, the Loyalists 'move heaven and earth to secure and put yourselves in status quo by the impoverishment and ruin of others.' What meant the welfare of commerce or the sanctity of treaties to such people? 'Go on Sirs,' they were admonished, 'until you have made yourselves as thoroughly odious to all ranks in this kingdom, as you are in

America.[27] When the wretched Loyalist returned to the attack, he drew upon himself additional condemnations including that of the powerful Committee of Merchants trading to North America.

The manifest contempt and brutality of 'Plain Truth's' enemies and the absence of a single voice raised in defence of the refugees run directly counter to allegations of Loyalist influence on British policy. John Adams' fears and suspicions, shared by so many of his fellow citizens, reflected frustration and disappointment and the need for a face-saving rationalization of American diplomatic failure.

To rule out significant Loyalist influence in the active shaping of British policy is not to state that the Loyalist issue was without a considerable importance in post-war Anglo-American relations. American mistreatment of the King's supporters furnished firm ground for Britain's complaint that the United States had been the first to violate the Treaty of Peace.

In America, war-born rancour and hatred made a mock of the Loyalist articles. The case is too well-established to require extensive exposition. Reaction in the southern states was especially violent. Ravaged by the war and owing vast sums to British merchants, an irate citizenry used every means—physical assault, intimidation, threats, riots, tar and feathers—to prevent the return of the exiles. In some states, new acts of banishment, some of which survived the War of 1812, closed the borders to large number of Loyalists.[28]

In the north, New York and Massachusetts furnished notable examples of continuing persecution of Loyalists, though proceedings at law were the usual mode, not physical violence. The New York Trespass Act, in particular brought on a 'carnival of spoliation' and a 'Tory witch-hunt'.[29]

Even Loyalists who did not attempt to return to America, but sought through agents to retrieve something from shattered estates, found the treaty's stipulations ignored. Venerable Harrison Gray, for example, sometime of Boston, was attainted and exiled by the revolutionary state government and his property confiscated. 'Patriot' debtors, to whom he had extended credit in happier days, immediately refused him payment. Subsisting on a British pension of £200 a year, he looked to

Article V of the treaty of peace for recourse in the recovery of his American debts. Pursuing his cause in the courts of Massachusetts, he found the defendants immediately relieved on the plea that he was an 'outlawed Tory'. There the matter could easily have rested, had not his grandson, Harrison Gray Otis, whose loyalty to the new regime was unimpeachable, put family above politics. Receiving assignments of the debts, he proceeded to sue successfully in his own name. The collusion ultimately recovered much of the £8000 due; but the process was long, arduous, and embittering.[30] Few refugees could have matched the relatively happy issue of Gray's troubles. Judicial discrimination, tar and feathers, the whip's thirteen stripes across the bare back, mob assaults, and even lynchings were not uncommon forms of treatment for Loyalists seeking restitution of their losses.

Many responsible Americans—among them Alexander Hamilton and John Jay—stood aghast at the scene. 'Instead of wholesome regulations for the improvement of our polity and commerce', Hamilton wrote to Gouverneur Morris, 'we are labouring to contrive methods to mortify and punish tories and to explain away treaties.' His father-in-law, General Schuyler, inveighed, too, against the actions of people who had 'hardly been emancipated from a threatened tyranny, forgetting how odious oppression appeared to them', before they began 'to play the tyrant, and give a melancholy evidence, that however capable we were of bearing adversity with magnanimity, we are too weak to support, with propriety, the prosperity we have so happily experienced.[31]

American representatives abroad were hard put to it to defend or palliate their countrymen's treatment of the Loyalists, and they were painfully aware of the condemnation general throughout Europe. John Jay in Paris wrote home in alarm, advising the Republic to act with greater humanity. Excepting only 'the faithless and the cruel', he would pardon all who had fought openly and honourably, or who had fled timidly before the storm. Exerting himself to minimize the violence and his country's responsibility for it, Franklin assured 'My dear Friend' David Hartley of the 'moderate disposition' entertained by Congress towards the Loyalists. The persecutions were not

due to the central government, President Boudinot informed
Franklin in a letter which the American passed on to Hartley,
but to Britain's prolonged occupation of New York and to
the 'Cruelties, Ravages, and Barbarities' committed by the
Loyalists themselves during the war. Newly arrived home
from Europe, Jay wasted little time in assuring British corre-
spondents that he had 'met with whigs and tories at the same
table'.[32]

The grim truth, however, could not be hidden. There
remained the flood of reports both from eyewitnesses and from
the sufferers themselves: in virtually every state of the Union,
the loyalist provisions of the treaty were flagrantly ignored and
local authorities in many states complacently acquiesced
in continuing persecutions. In Britain, it was clear that the
United States government was unable to impose its will on its
constituents, a fact which might explain but did not excuse
the breach of the treaty of peace from its inception. Here, for
them, was the 'prior infraction' which made all of Secretary
Jefferson's subsequent logic-chopping around the issue appear
both absurd and mendacious.

It was, then, not the Loyalists who used British policy; the
makers of British policy used the Loyalists—at least the issue
they represented—in the diplomatic contest which culminated
finally in the Jay-Grenville Treaty of 1794 which did not even
mention them.

NOTES

1. A substantial portion of the material in this paper appeared originally in my
Aftermath of Revolution, Dallas, 1969, paperback edition; the Norton Library, New
York, 1971. The present treatment represents a reappraisal of the subject, however,
and a major re-organization and extension of earlier conclusions.

2. To Messrs. Budges and Waller, Nantes, 10 August 1782; Shelburne Mss.,
Clements Library, 35.

3. See for example, Ralph Izard to Thomas Jefferson, April 1784, *Jefferson
Papers*, ed. Julian P. Boyd, Princeton, 1905–, VII, 129–31.

4. Loughborough to Eden, 1 October 1782, B. M. Add. Mss. 34419, fols. 50–1.

5. Eden to Loughborough, 5 October 1782, ibid., fols. 55–6.

6. John Adams to Jefferson, 1 November 1785, Jefferson *Papers*, IX, 3–4; Adams

to Jay, 29 July 1785, John Adams, *The Life and Works of John Adams* (ed. C. F. Adams, 10 vols, Boston 1850–6, VIII, 288–9; 6 August 1785, ibid., pp. 289–91; 4 November 1785, ibid., pp. 335–7; and 3 December 1785, ibid., pp. 350–6. See, too, Gouverneur Morris to Washington, London, 18 September 1790, Jared Sparks, *Life of Gouverneur Morris*, 3 vols, Boston 1832, I, 44.

7. Quoted by Robert Livingstone Schuyler, *The Fall of the Old Colonial System*, London, 1945, p. 93.

8. Adams' approximation is in *Works*, x, 87. Nelson's appears in his *The American Tory*, Oxford, p. 92. See also Wallace Brown, *The King's Friends*, Providence, R.I., 1965, pp. 280, 252.

9. xxv, April 1968, 29–77.

10. John Fiske, *Critical Period of American History*, Boston, 1888, p. 130. Arthur Granville Bradley, *Colonial Americans in Exile*, New York 1932, p. 108.

11. This point is developed more fully below.

12. Nelson, *The American Tory*, p. 153.

13. Galloway to Hardwicke, 19 November 1783, B.M. Add. MSS. 35621, fols. 202–3; 16 December 1783, ibid., fols. 258–9.

14. Quoted in Nelson, *The American Tory*, p. 159.

15. Vincent T. Harlow, *The Founding of the Second British Empire, 1763–1793*, London, 1952, p. 468 n. 31.

16. *British Colonial Government after the American Revolution*, New Haven, Conn., 1944, p. 44.

17. Simcoe to Undersecretary Evan Nepean, 16 March 1791, in E. A. Cruikshank (ed.), *The Correspondence of Lieutenant Governor John Graves Simcoe, with Allied Documents*, 5 vols, Toronto, 1923–31, I, 21.

18. *Morning Herald*, 20 March 1783; 'Arion', *Morning Chronicle*, 6 September 1783; and 'An Impartial Englishman', ibid., 25 October 1783.

19. Grace A. Cockcroft, *Public Life of George Chalmers*, New York, 1939, p. 62; *Parliamentary History*, XXIII, 1041; Manning, *British Colonial Government*, p. 39; Bradley, *Colonial Americans in Exile*, p. 108; *Parliamentary History*, XXVII, 1788–9; John Holland Rose, *William Pitt and National Revival*, London, 1911, pp. 444–5 and n.

20. 16 September 1783.

21. 18 November 1782, Shelburne MSS., Clements Library, 69, 203–6. Leslie's operation had in hand about 8000 refugees including both Whites and Negroes.

22. Vaughn to Shelburne, Paris, 1 November 1782, Vaughn MSS., Emmons Transcripts, Clements Library; Morgan to Shelburne, 12 June 1782, Shelburne MSS., Clements Library, 68, 373–87.

23. Public Records Office, Treasury Papers, 79, Report of 3 April 1790, P.R.O., Foreign Office 418.

24. Adams to John Jay, London, 19 April 1787, Adams, *Works*, VIII, 438.

25. B.M. Add. MSS. 38211, fol. 334.

26. 28 April 1787. See further my 'The London Press and the First Decade of American Independence', *Journal of British Studies*, 2, May 1963, pp. 105–7.

27. 30 May 1787, and ibid., p. 106 n. 61.

28. Merrell Jensen, *The New Nation*, New York, 1950, pp. 226–9; Nelson, *American Tory*, p. 166; John Randolph to Jefferson, Richmond, 24 April 1784, *Jefferson Papers*, VII, 116–17; Isaac S. Harrell, *Loyalism in Virginia*, Philadelphia 1926, pp. 137–8.

29. John Chester Miller, *Alexander Hamilton*, New York, 1959, pp. 103–4; Fiske, *Critical Period*, p. 124.

30. Samuel Eliot Morison, *The Life and Letters of Harrison Gray Otis, Federalist*, 2 vols, Boston, 1913, I, 38–9.

31. Hamilton to Morris, New York, 21 February 1784, Hamilton MSS., Library of Congress; Schuyler to John Jay, 18 February 1784, William Jay, *Life of John Jay*, 2 vols, New York, 1833, II, 148–50.

32. Jay to R. R. Livingston, 19 July 1783, W. Jay, *Life of John Jay*, I, 174–81, and 12 September 1783, ibid., II, 127–8. See my *Aftermath of Revolution*, p. 424 n. 38. enclosing a copy of the 'very curious bill'.

Loyalists, Whigs and the Idea of Equality

J. R. POLE

The United States began its independent existence with an unusually formal pronouncement of moral principle. The doctrine that all men are created equal is undoubtedly both the most celebrated and the most controversial pronouncement in the preamble to the Declaration of Independence. In the form which it assumed at the hands of Thomas Jefferson, the statement drew upon the general theory of natural rights, which had an ancient lineage in the history of both political and religious thought. However unclear or ambiguous that doctrine may have been, in view particularly of the obvious reservations in the commitments of many of its actual signatories, the Declaration certainly had the effect of increasing the number of people who applied the concept of equality to themselves. It gave the full sanction of the national purpose of the new Republic to an idea that was to prove itself one of the most potent in the history of political thought.

These impressive consequences have a natural tendency to lead the mind back to the intentions behind the Declaration. When Jefferson and his colleagues dedicated themselves to the rhetoric of the preamble, they assumed a wider brief than had strictly been conferred on them by the Continental Congress. The colonial dispute with Britain did involve the problem of equality, in a form that was of the most acute significance; but the issues could have been defined in a far more limited and legalistic manner without impairing the colonial case and without offending the social susceptibilities of large numbers of American owners of slaves and indentured servants.

Americans of varying interests and political persuasions were able to agree on the main grounds of the American argument until a late stage in the proceedings of the Continental Congress. When separation came, it divided men who had always held remarkably similar views about the place of Americans under British law, and the equality which was due to them by the fundamental principles of that law. Among such men, a striking example, because of his acknowledged political and social conservatism, was Joseph Galloway. Galloway's long association with Franklin in the politics of Pennsylvania began to break down some time after the passage of the Townshend Tariff Act when the two men differed seriously about the constitutionality of the parliamentary legislation that was being imposed on the American colonies.[1] Yet at an early date in the proceedings of the Continental Congress, 8 September 1774, Galloway made a speech whose argument had much in common with the conventional principles of the American Whigs or patriots. 'I never could find the rights of Americans in the distinction between taxation and legislation, nor in the distinction between laws for revenue and for the regulation of trade', he said; 'I have looked for our rights in the state of nature, but could not find them in the state of nature, but always in a state of political society...I have looked for them in the constitution of the English government, and there found them. We may draw them from this source securely.' He went on to say that power resulted from the real property of society and, like those of Greece, Macedon and Rome, the English constitution was founded on the same principle. He held it to be the essence of the English constitution that no laws were binding but such as were made by the consent of the proprietors in England. From all of which he concluded that the American settlers ceased to be bound by parliamentary statutes when they came to America; so that all subsequent acts of Parliament controlling the colonies were violations of their rights.[2]

This does not sound like the language of a man who was soon to become an American Tory. Not, as a matter of fact, that Galloway's ground was the same as that of many colonial spokesmen. But he did share with them the vitally important view that Parliament possessed no rights over the internal life of the colonies. Whatever the differences of approach, Galloway stood here on Whig principles. Yet it was Galloway who was most earnestly committed to saving the Empire and who proposed a rational Plan of Union that might even have succeeded in doing so. Neither from his interpretation of the nature of the Empire, nor on his record as a Pennsylvania politician, would it have been easy to say which side he would eventually take. Galloway always tended to see social problems in terms of order and authority; he was not interested in remoulding society, only in getting the relationship with Britain right; in his own province he had been involved for years in the plan to transfer the proprietorship to the Crown. Daniel Dulany of Maryland, another American who was eventually to take his side with the Crown, had spoken in comparable language when the Stamp Act was at issue nine years earlier. In his *Considerations on the Propriety of Imposing Taxes in the Colonies* (1765) Dulany fired one of the early shots in the American controversy with Britain when he argued the claim of the colonists to exemption from all taxes imposed without their consent as British subjects. This right they derived from the common law, which their charters had both declared and confirmed. Dulany, on the other hand, gave a hint of the intellectual difficulties that lay in store for those who wanted to retain the existing theory of sovereignty when he said that the colonists acknowledged themselves as subordinate to the mother country. His admission of this subordination was if anything even more fervent than that of James Otis.[3]

This mention of the common law was significant. The common law was the basic source of the English conception of rights. By tracing it we can observe the contradictions that were to develop in the position of men who conceived of themselves both as English Whigs and American Whigs, as loyal subjects and as patriotic Americans. According to Martin Howard Jr., of Rhode Island, in his *Letter from a Gentleman at Halifax* (Newport, 1765), personal rights were to be distinguished from political rights, and personal rights were secured by common law, which were every subject's birthright. But the political rights of the colonies were more limited and depended on their charters; in his view, the colonies enjoyed no rights independent of their charters. Howard was defending British policies, and in a spirit almost exactly opposite to that of Galloway in 1774, he asserted that the jurisdiction of Parliament over the colonies derived from common law, which was the constitution of

England. Like Galloway, he held that attendance in Parliament was originally a duty arising from tenure of land; and hence the privilege of representation was territorial, and was therefore confined to Britain alone.

Howard and Galloway thus drew opposite conclusions from the same premise. The common law was fundamental, representation was based on land; but Howard concluded that the common law came first, so that parliamentary powers were legal and legitimate because they drew their strength from the basis of common law. These assumptions did not yet clearly indicate the distinctions that would arise between future Tories and future Whigs; yet they do show that those who held them, when faced with British policies that made reconciliation an impossibility within the old imperial structure, could sever themselves from British sovereignty while remaining true to what they had always considered to be their fundamental constitutional principles. Others would find it possible to hold to the same principles without separating themselves in the last resort from British supremacy. There was, perhaps, no wholly satisfactory logical resolution to the dilemma. Yet the similarity of principles among American spokesmen, most of whom had some claim to speak as lawyers, gives a very significant indication of the extent and character of the legal and moral concepts which they applied to their own society. These views were based on ancient laws traced through English and colonial history; they could hardly have been expected to give rise to the resounding affirmation of the principles of equality which America addressed to the opinions of mankind in July 1776.

A discussion of the meaning of the ideas of equality in the Declaration of Independence must distinguish between those ideas and the more limited meaning attached to equality throughout the phases of the legal controversy with Britain in the preceding years. The preamble placed American independence squarely on a declared foundation of equally derived natural rights, in which Americans would thenceforth have a moral claim to equal shares. Yet the phraseology of the preamble was not as unambiguous as it has often seemed to succeeding generations, and it might not have gained the assent of so many contemporaries if they had read it in the light of its later and more radical interpretation. It will therefore not be out of place to ask exactly what it meant to those who signed it. The preamble describes its own central proposition as 'self-evident'. But what does that mean? The Declaration of Independence was not issued with an accompanying glossary of philosophical terms, and it is by no means certain that the meaning of the phrase 'self-evident' is, itself, evident. Fortunately Jefferson's own earlier drafts come to our help. It appears from the Rough Draft that Jefferson himself intended to describe these truths as 'sacred and undeniable', and that the alteration to 'self-evident' is in a hand that resembles Franklin's.[5] This alteration suggests something more than a preference in choice of words; like all significant changes in literary style, it conveys a different meaning. Jefferson's own use of the word 'sacred' may have implied only an echo of the idea that the human capacity for knowledge was implanted by divine power, but it does bear a direct reference to that power. There is a difference between rights that are sacred, like the divine right of kings, and rights that are secular, like those embodied in the writ of habeas corpus. Small though this change may have been —and for all we know, Jefferson may have accepted it without the murmurs that he raised about some of the others—it symbolizes the final transition from the theological to the secular basis of modern politics.

This statement may seem to need a little amplification. After all, John Locke, who could certainly number Jefferson among his American readers, had put his specifically political views on a primarily secular foundation. Yet Mr John Dunn has shown us that Locke's concept of human equality was fundamentally theological; it depended on the Calvinistic doctrine of the Calling.[6] 'The calling is thus a summons from God, but it is a summons for the interpretation of which each adult individual is fully responsible.'[7] This responsibility involved for each individual a continuous relationship with God; but the privacy of that relationship had very little to do with the structure of society. The theological basis of Jefferson's politics led to conclusions that were at least as secular as Locke's, and from the personal point of view, distinctly less religious. In his view, the equality of individuals, and the rights in which they shared as equals, derived from one single original act of creation. Having been imparted from their sacred source, they were undeniable, inherent, and in the nature of the case, inalienable; but they did not impose on each individual any express religious responsibility. Presumably it would also be true to say of Locke's views, as of Jefferson's, that an individual would not alienate his political rights by lapsing in his religious observances. But in Jefferson's case the emphasis is wholly secular, and the rights of the individual in no way continue to depend on, or even be known as a manifestation of, his personal relationship to God. The point is implied in the naturalistic way in which God is actually described. The laws on which America's separate and equal station depend are said to be those 'of nature and nature's God'. 'God's nature' might have been an implicitly more respectful way of describing the order in which creation had occurred, though it would have lacked a certain stylistic balance.

However these rights might have been originated, the term 'self-evident' is not quite self-explanatory. As it cannot mean that the truths in question are evident to themselves, it must be taken to mean 'evident to the senses'; which must include moral apprehension. Even if the overt meaning is 'evident on sight', this must clearly be so, for it is the mind, not the eye, that perceives truth. It follows that every member of the human race is provided with his own equipment of moral apprehension; and the statement can be of value only if it affirms a truth that applies universally. It declares that no one could be equipped with the normal moral sense without being accessible to the truth that all men are created equal. This puts us in a position to see—not, perhaps, for the first time, but the point seems worth confirming—why the Declaration of Independence was to be of such enormous potency. It told every individual that he was capable of seeing these things for himself. The analogy with religious doctrine was close, and significant because politics borrowed from its theological counterpart; the Calvinists and other religious instructors held that each person bore throughout his life a primary responsibility to God. In much the same way, the Declaration of Independence told people that each of them bore a responsibility for a continuous relationship to his government.

Nothing very concrete followed immediately from this statement. Individuals could carry these responsibilities quite adequately within the existing organization of government; state constitutions were made anew in the same period, but they were made generally on lines that continued and broadened that organization. The concept of consent was central to the case stated by the Declaration of Independence against the British, but that case did not involve a new relationship between rulers and ruled in American society. The Declaration rested on principles too general to imply specific institutional consequences; and, moreover, these principles, when subjected to exegesis, soon disclosed the presence of underlying ambiguities. It appeared that different individuals did have different moral apprehensions. The first difficulty arose, in the committee delegated to produce a draft declaration, over Jefferson's denunciation of the slave trade, which is not the less celebrated for having been suppressed. Since the problems of equality between whites and Negroes were ideological as well as practical, and since slavery was an existing institution, it will hardly be a digression to take note of Jefferson's own formulation in 1776. In the first place, it was the slave trade rather than slavery itself against which Jefferson's fire was directed. Slavery might be thought to be subsumed under the slave trade, but the failure to draw this distinction became widespread, and made it possible for persons of humanitarian sentiment to discharge their feelings of revolted justice without endangering their subsistence. In the indictment against George III, which was the form taken by Jefferson's attack on the slave trade, the blame for American slavery was itself laid squarely, if not fairly, at the door of the British. Jefferson concluded, with a minimum of cost to his compatriots, by denouncing the British administration for inciting the enslaved Negroes to rise against their American masters, who emerged as the unwilling victims of this complicated plot.[8] Jefferson's colleagues, however, held that his language was too provocative for the Congress, and the entire passage was dropped. They could not so easily rid their country of the moral issue, and even in its suppressed form, Jefferson's statement was to have indefinite future reverberations.

The passages that were approved are not free from their own

problems of interpretation, which suggest at least three possible readings. Taking these in the order in which they seem to have taken shape, which is not necessarily a logical order, the first interpretation is that all individuals who belong to a single community, or system of laws, ought to be considered as equals within it. The historical significance of this reading is that the Americans believed that they did belong to such a community, the British Empire, within which, according to its own rules, they had rights to equal treatment. It was the failure of this interpretation, the violation of its tenets by successive British governments, that drove the Americans into the position at which the second reading comes to be formulated. This is that any one people, considered collectively as a self-identified group, possesses in that capacity the same rights as any other people. British policy forced the Americans to adopt this position, and once granted that the Americans constituted such a people, it followed that the British could no more make laws to govern the Americans than the Americans themselves could make laws to govern Britain—or, to take a popular example, than the Scottish Parliament before the Act of Union could govern England. Some Americans saw this point very early, but the majority took several years of a struggle that was plainly psychological as well as political before they reached this conclusion. Yet there are good reasons for thinking that, once the first proposition had broken down because of British intransigeance, it was a principle which Jefferson and his colleagues would have accepted as a sufficient statement of their practical meaning. Jefferson's own *Summary View of the Rights of British America* had recently made the same point; the American provincial legislatures were thus seen to be sovereign within their own colonies as Parliament was sovereign in Britain, and neither had any authority to reach out and control the other. Similar opinions had been expressed over several years of colonial protests by those who had dared to think right through the logical difficulties in the way of the American claims. Moreover, the opening sentences of the Declaration of Independence referred specifically to the separation of one people from another and to their assumptions of a 'separate and equal station'. That was the practical issue, and it was to justify that step that Congress made its appeal to 'the opinions of mankind'.[9]

The third reading is much the most radical. It can be put simply by saying that all individuals, everywhere, and at all times, possess equal rights to these benefits; so that every infringement that has ever occurred, ancient, medieval or modern, was a deprivation of natural rights. an infraction of the laws of nature. The fact that these rights were believed to derive from a single creation gives this final view a certain compulsive force. It makes the American declaration an example to the world. But, on the practical side, it did not impose upon the Americans any obligation to act beyond the boundaries of their own legislative competence. (Their practical attempt to do so, for the benefit of the people of Canada, had already proved a dismal failure.) The distinction between these three interpretations should not be taken as rigid or exclusive. But the first reading contained all that Americans needed to say about their rights or about theories of equality in their quarrel with Britain so long as they remained within the Empire and had some hope of making an effective defence of their liberties. This phase of the argument was too firmly rooted in constitutional ground to give occasion for any spacious appeals to natural rights; the rights that belonged to Americans by nature were their rights as true, or natural-born, Englishmen, and the assertion of these rights involved all that Americans needed to claim about equality. The connections between these ideas were explained by the learned Virginian Richard Bland, in his pamphlet, *An Enquiry into the Rights of the British Colonies*, which appeared in 1769, when Americans were concerting their resistance to the Townshend duties. 'I am speaking of the *rights* of a people: *rights* imply *equality*, in the instances to which they belong...By what *right* is it, that the parliament can exercise such a power over the colonies, who have as natural a right to the privileges and liberties of *Englishmen*, as if they were actually resident within the Kingdom?'[10]

The instances to which these rights pertained obviously included all the issues between the colonists and Britain. The unequal treatment of which they complained was specific, and the colonial protests, from the time of the local question of writs of assistance in Massachusetts in 1760–1, to the last appeals of the years 1774–6, do not rely for the force of their arguments on general ideas of equality. General ideas were certainly present, because it was their correspondence with natural rights that gave to English constitutional and common laws their peculiar distinction. But, as Otis said, 'The truth is, as has been shown, men come into the world and into society at the same instant.' Natural and original rights could best 'be illustrated and explained' by the abstraction of a state of nature; but they were living under civil law.[11] The question, what would happen if English law departed from natural law, simply did not arise; the whole problem was created by British administrative and parliamentary acts which departed from the precepts of the constitution and common law. Otis significantly dismissed Grotius and Pufendorf and drew his sentiments from 'our English writers, particularly from Mr. *Locke*, to whom might be added a *few* of other nations...'[12] The actual substance of the American claim was to an equality of specified rights; and these threatened rights, which eventually the Americans were prepared to defend with their lives, were in very large degree their rights at common law. It was by virtue of the deprivation of common law rights that they were made aware of the problem of inequality, and during the prolonged quarrel with Britain this was the only active sense in which the concept of equality made itself felt.

This is not to say that no other or wider ideas of equality were abroad in America. Such a statement would give a quite false impression of the fluidity of many aspects of society, of the expectations of many of its members, and of the declarations of a variety of persons including some at least of the clergy. John Woolman had disturbed the consciences of slaveowners, and the Quakers had already begun to condemn slavery. There were rough but reverberant notes of both spiritual and social equality sounding in the religious revivals and in the social conditions that governed many American lives. But these sentiments were not translated into any of the formal statements used in the arguments over American rights. These arguments, being directed against allegedly unconstitutional assumptions of parliamentary power over the property of subjects, were quite adequately served by references to constitutional principles; they did not in principle call for the support of natural rights. The statement that the Americans, in their argument with Britain, were not concerned with the enunciation of general ideas of equality in the more elementary sense might therefore be considered as a historical truism; the colonial polemics would in this sense simply be the wrong place to look for such ideas, and the relative silence of colonial pamphlets would not necessarily lead to the inference that ideas of equality did not exist or were of no force.

But this would be a narrow view, even of that most enigmatic of sources, the evidence of silence. Americans did have ideas as to what they were entitled to *by nature*; and Bland's revealing expression showed that the rights to which they were naturally entitled were those they inherited by virtue of being Englishmen by birth—that is, natural-born Englishmen. These rights, embodied in the common law, gave all the protection that they needed. Their more general expressions were sounded in the invocation of liberty, a far more highly treasured English right than equality. The English—now the British—Constitution was all that men could need for their protection in society precisely because it incorporated all the liberty that could stand the social state. Any possible theme of equality was quite necessarily subordinate to this principle, and was complete with the doctrine of equality before the law, which, under the stress of political exigencies, would emerge as equality in common law rights. In due course—the course of human events—the Americans were soon to remodel the constitutions of their provinces into those of independent states. In going about this work the leaders of the various American societies expressed the egalitarian impulses that existed in those societies only within a framework that owed its dominant characteristics to traditional institutions. The new state constitutions made numerous adjustments and reforms, of which the most important were extensions of the suffrage, and the introduction of the majority principle as the normal basis of representation;[13] they clearly carried the demand for equality as far as it could be made to go in American political life while remaining compatible with the other beliefs and interests of the revolutionary era. But these developments have to be considered in the light of the impulse already imparted by the Declaration of Independence and by the grave resolves undertaken by the Americans. Even so, the new laws and constitutions retained many layers of institutional protection for interests whose preservation was thought to be one of the main legitimate reasons for the existence of social organization—property, in its various manifestations, being the most important. The American Revolution ushered into existence an egalitarian rhetoric, but not an egalitarian society.

The declarations of rights in these state constitutions enacted, or at least proclaimed, the more important provisions of the common law rights of Englishmen. During the harrowing years of intermittent controversy with Britain, future Loyalists had essentially concurred with future Whigs that the common law was crucial to their rights. Yet those who had not had the opportunity of reading Blackstone might reasonably have been forgiven for a certain vagueness about the origins and peculiar character of the common law, which owed its name to its origin as the law that was common to the whole kingdom. In the twelfth-century patchwork of jurisdictions and liberties, including those of different regions, of feudal barons and of the ecclesiastical courts, King Henry II at the Assizes of Clarendon, 1166 and Northampton, 1176, did much to consolidate the governing principle of a general law that would obtain anywhere in his realms. Common law was case law.[14] It developed from precedent to precedent and by extension, or extrapolation, from case to case. Its principles were thus independent of statutes, though statute law could take over and occupy ground previously held by common law. In a conflict, statute law would prevail; but where a statute abrogated a section of the common law, the common law courts would be likely to hold that the statute constituted an exception; they would be unlikely to proceed to reinterpret related common law cases in the light of the statute, in a case where they could choose the path of applying it only to the issue to which it specifically applied. No element of the English constitution was thought to be more fundamental than the common law, which is why it was possible for James Otis to argue that it was superior to and could control statute law;[15] he had got the point wrong, but it would on the whole have been true, as suggested, that the courts would normally attempt to interpret statutes in a manner consistent with common law rather than in opposition to it. The statement that no part of the Constitution was more fundamental than the common law implies that they were continuous with each other; the most prominent of the colonial grievances, taxation without representation, was not less an example of this continuity of principle by virtue of the fact that taxes were raised in Parliament. The absoluteness of a man's right to his property was a basic common law right; that was why only the owner, or his appointed deputy, could grant any portion of his property to the king. The first serious encroachments on the common law rights of the colonists, or at any rate the first serious challenge to such encroachments, arose in connection with writs of assistance in Massachusetts, whose character very closely resembled those of general warrants. The question of general warrants came to a head shortly afterwards in Britain and gave rise to some of the most celebrated decisions in British constitutional history. The closeness of the issues and the fact that the outcome was different in the colonies from the mother country was not lost on the Americans, and makes both sides of the story an object of attention.

In Massachusetts, Governor Shirley had issued writs of assistance to customs officers as a legal protection against lawsuits or physical resistance. The writ—usually written at the time as a writ of 'assistants'—was so called because it instructed constables or other officers to give assistance to customs officers in the execution of their duties. In 1755, the Superior Court assumed responsibility for the issue of these writs in Massachusetts. Since the writs were not returnable to the court of issue after the execution of a specified task, but remained valid during the lifetime of the reigning monarch, the authority delegated in this way could be extremely broad. When drawn in this form the writ of assistance constituted a virulent species of general warrant. However, all things done in the king's name, including legislative assemblies or parliaments summoned, and writs issued, came to an end within six months after the monarch's death; so that the death of King George II in October 1760 gave the merchants of Boston the opportunity of arranging to oppose the renewed issue of the detested writs in the new reign. The case was heard before Chief Justice Thomas Hutchinson and his colleagues in the Superior Court, the merchants being represented by James Otis Jr, and Oxenbridge Thatcher.[16]

Both Thatcher and Otis denounced the non-returnability of the writs, which became a grant of unlimited power over people's homes. The common law principle that an Englishman's home is his castle was no mere cliché but a strict article of the case; and Thatcher argued further that the Act of Parliament authorizing this kind of writ gave the power of issue only to the Court of Exchequer in England, to which the Massachusetts Superior Court was not the equivalent. According to John Adams's well-known report,[17] written out some time after the hearings, Otis proceeded to a fiery denuciation of the tyrannical power granted by these virtually unlimited writs. He admitted that the old books gave certain precedents for general warrants, but 'in more modern books you will find only special warrants to search such and such houses specially named, in which the complainant has before sworn that he suspects his goods are concealed; and you will find it adjudged that special warrants only are legal'. It was precisely because it was general that the writ prayed for was illegal. Otis went further and declared, as he was to do in later pamphlets, that an act against the constitution was void. Officers of the plantations had the same powers, but under the same limits, as those at home.

These arguments, with the exception of Otis's general proposition about acts against the constitution, were in substance to be vindicated soon afterwards by the English Court of Common Pleas. Chief Justice Hutchinson, however, was not persuaded, and prevailed on the bench to defer their decision until the English practice could be ascertained, for which purpose Hutchinson wrote, not to the English attorney-general, but to the Massachusetts agent in London, William Bollan. Bollan satisfied the court that it had the requisite powers, and accordingly the case ended with the renewed issue of writs of assistance late in 1761.[18] This was the close of the immediate story in the Bay Colony. The Assembly angrily discharged Bollan from his agency, but the issue does not seem to have been re-opened. This, however, was not the end of colonial opposition to writs of assistance; but processes which the colonists could hardly regard as mere accidental concatenations of circumstance soon set similar acts of oppression in motion in England, but with an outcome of deeply significant difference.

An administration that enjoyed little respect and perhaps lacked confidence in itself was stung by the virulent satire of John Wilkes, M.P. for Aylesbury, through his paper, *The North Briton*. Number Forty-five of this paper contained statements which the Secretary of State, the Earl of Halifax, condemned as seditious libel, for which he decided to prosecute. He therefore issued a general warrant, 'to make strict and diligent search for the authors, printers, and publishers of a seditious and treasonable paper entitled, The North Briton, No. 45...and them, or any of them, to apprehend and seize, together with their papers'. It is to be noticed that no one was named in this warrant, under which forty-nine persons, including the journeymen printers, were arrested in three days. The printers were held for only six hours; but Wilkes, who was taken for interrogation by the secretaries of state, whom he appears to have treated with the utmost contempt, spent six days in the Tower. Meanwhile his papers were rifled by Robert Wood, Lord Halifax's secretary. Another victim of a similar warrant was John Entick, author of another allegedly seditious paper, against whom the writ was specific as to person but general as to papers, and who began a separate action against Nathan Carrington, the king's messenger who had carried out the search. Wilkes and the journeymen printers began their own actions, all being heard in the Court of Common Pleas, and leading to the celebrated judgments in *Wilkes* v. *Wood*, better known as the *Case of General Warrants* (1763); and Entick's separate action led to *Entick* v. *Carrington* (1765).[19]

The figure who dominated these events was the best friend that the American colonists themselves possessed in Britain throughout the entire period. The views and public pronouncements of Charles Pratt, Chief Justice of the Common Pleas, form a perfect unity of the English and the American interests in the protection of the basic common law liberties of English subjects. He is better known to history, through his elevation to the peerage, as Lord Chief Justice Camden, in which capacity he continued to defend Whig principles of the old kind when they came under attack in the quarrel with the American colonies. Camden does not seem to have wavered in his defence of colonial interests. In 1766 he used his new seat in the House of Lords to denounce the Declaratory Act as a bill 'the very existence of which is illegal, absolutely illegal, contrary to the fundamental laws of nature, contrary to the fundamental laws of this kingdom'. Taxation and representation, according to a doctrine as old as the constitution, were 'inseparably united'.[20] Americans were informed of Camden's endeavours in their defence through their newspapers, which several years later reported over the Boston Port Bill that 'Lord Camden exerted himself nobly in the House of Lords'.[21] In the summer of 1775 Camden was reported as defending the Americans on the principles of the Revolution—meaning, of course, that of 1688. 'To say that no violation of charters, no infraction of civil compacts, no erasure of rights would justify resistance, was to give up the cause of the revolution,' he told the Lords, and concluded: 'As an Englishman I cannot wish harm to my mother country; but I wish most sincerely that the Americans may *preserve their liberty*.'[22]

English liberties were the ones at issue in the cases involving general warrants, though they were not the less American for being English. In giving his judgment in Wilkes's case, the Chief Justice explained the nature of the issue:

His Lordship then went upon the warrant, which he declared was a point of the greatest consequence he ever met with in his whole practice. The defendents claimed a right, under precedents, to force persons' houses, break open escrutores, seize their papers, etc., upon a general warrant, where no inventory is made of the things thus taken away, and where no offenders' names are specified in the warrant, and therefore a discretionary power given to messengers to search wherever their suspicious may chance to fall. If such a power is truly invested in a Secretary of State, and he can delegate this power, it may certainly affect the person and property of every man in this kingdom, and is totally subversive of the liberty of the subject.[23]

Wilkes, who had sued for £5000 damages, was awarded £1000, an extraordinary sum to be awarded against a secretary of state; the journeymen printers received varying sums of £200 to £300 for their lesser injuries, but these damages, awarded to working men against the government's officers, marked a notable vindication of the liberties of British subjects no matter what their rank. The case of *Entick* v. *Carrington* gave the occasion for an even more resounding rebuke to the administration, which the Lord Chief Justice founded firmly on the common law of England, remarking at one point that he could have wished upon this occasion that the Revolution had not been considered the only basis for their liberties. The point was that the Revolution restored the Constitution to its original principles. He put great emphasis on the authority of the books of common law: 'If it be law, it will be found in our books. If it is not to be found there, it is not law.' This observation was taken up when he came to the question of whether a publication could be censored, as had been done under the Licensing Act of Charles II, or could only be made the subject of a subsequent prosecution:

It is then said, that it is necessary for the ends of government to lodge such a power with a state officer; that it is better to prevent such a publication before, than to punish the offender afterwards. I answer, that if the legislature be of that opinion they will revive the Licensing Act. But if they have not done that, I conceive they are not of that opinion. And with respect to the argument of state necessity, or a distinction that has been aimed at between state offences and others, the common law does not understand that kind of reasoning, nor do our books take notice of any such distinctions.[24]

It is reported that Camden burnt his own copy of this judgment because he did not think it worthy of preservation, and that the record is due to notes taken by a friend of his. When the administration appealed the printers' case to the King's Bench, Lord Mansfield, Lord Chief Justice of the King's Bench, affirmed judgment for the printer of No. Forty-five of the *North Briton*. Mansfield agreed with Camden as to the law, but did not have Camden's taste for rhetoric. In the immediate aftermath, the House of Commons resolved that general warrants were illegal, a step which drew something of a rebuke from Lord Mansfield, who stated in the Lords that if Parliament could declare general warrants illegal it could presumably declare them legal, but he would hold them to be illegal whatever either House of Parliament might say![25]

Camden's judgments in these cases gave him an immense popularity. Toasts were drunk, the freedom of cities conferred, portraits painted (Dr Johnson even wrote an inscription for one of them); and—a significant mark of favour in England—taverns were named after him. In 1766 Camden became Lord Chancellor in Chatham's administration, an office he held until 1768.

These events were closely followed in the American colonies. All the leading cases, not to mention a great many other adventures in the life of Wilkes, were reported in the American press, except that of *Entick* v. *Carrington*, which got little attention; this neglect may have been due to the fact that the issues had already been settled in the earlier cases, and to the growing preoccupation with the Stamp Act. Most of the reports from England were printed first in the principal newspapers where they were received and were then copied verbatim in other parts of the colonies; so that if a small number of editors failed to pick up the reports, the effect would be that of widespread neglect. But Camden's fame in America makes clear that colonial readers were keenly aware of the issues. When the Stamp Act was repealed, Camden held a high place of honour in the numerous toasts and celebrations; the press carried frequent favourable references to his conduct and principles. Most significant of American favour was the naming of towns and counties, which still bear testimony to America's gratitude to the great English Whig judge of their time.[26]

The judgments making general warrants illegal in England had important implications for the colonies, which were not lost on the English attorney-general, William De Grey, who in October 1766 advised the customs commissioners to use a strict construction of the statute of William III under which they had been entering houses and warehouses. By this he meant that they were to act with very great restraint. The obvious inference was that such searches and seizures had been illegal, and care was taken to keep De Grey's advice secret.[27] The difficulty caused by the English rulings was remedied by the

Townshend Act, which in addition to its tariff provisions included a clause which formally legalized the American writs of assistance and designated the superior court of each province as the court of issue. When the House of Commons had condemned general warrants it has excepted such cases as might be provided for by act of Parliament, thus giving itself freedom for future action of which in this way it soon took advantage. Nothing could more forcibly have demonstrated for the benefit of Americans the fact that in Parliament's view they did not share equally in the rights and privileges which protected the liberties and properties of Englishmen at home.[28]

The Townshend provision caused acute difficulties for American judges, but found them, on the whole, in remarkably consistent array against the issue of writs of assistance on a general basis. Requests for such writs from the customs collectors started to reach the courts in 1768 and were repeated, in face of a steady, if often anxious, series of rejections by the bench. In nine of the colonies—including the Floridas—the judges considered and refused these requests, despite English pressure, to which De Grey added the force of his authority. The answer of Chief Justice William Allen of Pennsylvania to John Swift, collector of the port of Philadelphia, was characteristic:

Sir,

I have duly considered the application you made to grant you a Writ of Assistants. Though my duty and my inclination would lead me to do everything in my power to promote the King's service, yet I conceive that I am not Warranted by Law to issue any such Warrant. But not being willing to trust to my own judgement entirely, I have laid the matter before the Attorney General and another eminent lawyer who both concur with me in opinion that such a general writ as you have demanded is not agreeeble to Law.

I beg leave to assure you I am

Sir
Your Obedient Humble Servant
Will Allen.

The issue was pressed hardest by the Crown in Virginia, where it was raised in 1769, 1772 and 1773; but the court firmly refused to grant the writs, and intimated on the final occasion that it did not wish to hear of them again. In South Carolina, on the other hand, after some years of resistance, the judges gave way as late as April 1773, though it is not known whether the court was persuaded by legal argument or by political pressure. Elsewhere the colonial position was one of determined resistance, based on the conviction that the writs were illegal under the English constitution; in Connecticut, Judge Trumbull consulted with judges in other colonies before giving an opinion, and it seems likely that this correspondence was intended to concert colonial resistance.[29]

Americans never lost sight of the central importance of freedom from official powers of unrestricted search and seizure. John Dickinson devoted a passage to the question in number ix of his *Letters from a Farmer in Pennsylvania*, drawing attention to the invidious distinction between Englishmen and Americans in respect of these rights;[30] Patrick Henry, in opposing the ratification of the federal Constitution, specifically attacked the omission of general warrants, particularly fatal in a vast country with 'no judge within a thousand miles to issue a writ of habeas corpus'.[31] This in spite of the fact that Virginia had included a prohibition expressly against general warrants. This provision became a common form in the new state constitutions; it was copied exactly by Pennsylvania and included by Massachusetts in the constitution of 1780.[32] It is significant that the Continental Congress's Declaration of Grievances of 14 October 1774 claimed 'That the respective colonies are entitled to the common law of England, and more especially to the great and inestimable privilege of being tried by their peers of the vicinage, according to the course of that law'.[33] The conclusion to the story of general warrants was written into the Federal Constitution with the adoption of the Fourth Amendment, which forbids 'unreasonable searches and seizures' and guarantees security to people in their homes; it may reasonably be said that this Amendment virtually enacts Lord Chief Justice Camden's opinions as the supreme law of the land, a point of which the judges, not to say the legislators, may still occasionally need to be reminded.

The Congressional Declaration referred to the right of Americans to be tried by their peers in the neighbourhood. This issue

constituted the other great grievance against unequal treatment. The jurisdiction of the vice-admiralty courts, which had
first been established in the colonies in the Navigation Act of
1696, emerged as a bitter American grievance after British
attempts to reorganize them in the 1760s. The first of these
occurred under the Revenue or Sugar Act of 1764, which
created the new court at Halifax. This court made little practical difference to colonial life because it transacted virtually
no business, but after an attempt to increase the number of such
courts, by the Stamp Act, had failed when that measure was
repealed, it was not until 1770 that a further attempt to create
an effective judicial authority led to the creation of four new
district courts. Vice-admiralty courts, equipped to deal with
technical questions of marine law, were popular with British
merchants, who did not wish to subject themselves to the inter-
minable complexities of common law in disputes that arose over
their transactions; but they operated without juries, and Americans began to perceive in the extension of this system one more
piece of evidence pointing to the British plan to reduce them to
slavery. The deprivation of the inestimable right of trials by juries
became one of the most insistently reiterated of the American
grievances, and reappeared in the Declaration of Independence.
It was not a deprivation from which many Americans suffered
serious inconvenience or injustice, but it attracted attention on
certain notorious occasions; the famous trial of John Hancock,
for the illegal unloading of his sloop *Liberty*, dragged on through
the winter of 1768–9, causing great weariness and misery to his
counsel, John Adams, but gaining public acclaim for both
Hancock and the cause for which his vessel was named. Adams
told the court that his client had never consented to the laws
under which he was being tried. It was yet another case of the
discrimination from which Americans now suffered.[34]

These issues turned ultimately on greater themes than those
that could be limited to common law. What was at stake was
the hegemony of the British Parliament over the American
colonies; and for Americans the question resolved itself into the
right of self-government, or as later generations would call it,
self-determination. Yet the question arose because common law
rights were denied. It was in that sense that the problem of

equality came to present itself to Americans as involving general principles of public policy, as opposed to the choices open to individuals or groups in their local arrangements. When in the course of the dispute with Britain the colonists were finally brought to the point of independence, the man to whom was delegated the task of drafting a declaration, on account of his well-known felicity of style, began his statement with a sweeping assertion of natural rights. Jefferson's was far from being the first assertion that the Americans' case rested ultimately on natural rights, but it was the first American pronouncement to make a prominent connection between such rights and the case for individual equality. The connection caused enough trouble in the Congress. But in Virginia the objections were still more awkward when the same claim was advanced in the Declaration of Rights attached to the proposed constitution. This declaration affirmed that 'all men are by nature equally free and independent'. Robert Carter Nicholas led an opposition which was reconciled somewhat grudgingly after being assured that the statement could not possibly be held to apply to Negroes because Negroes were not 'constituent members' of society.[35]

There is a logical sense in which this view was strictly consistent with the words employed by the Virginia Declaration, which said that all men had 'certain inherent rights, of which, when they enter into a state of society, they cannot by any compact deprive or divest their posterity...' It was arguable that the slaves had never entered into American society in the sense of that language. The whole concept, redolent as it was of traditional Lockean and Whig thinking, depended on a voluntaristic concept of social formation which was obviously missing from the beginning in the Negro relationship to white society. To say this is not to say that the language employed gave a philosophically satisfactory account of the rights and wrongs of the current situation. After all the social contract was basically a metaphor; but it was by making it into a literal statement that Jefferson's Virginian contemporaries were able to make it work for them as an instrument of current social policy.

On the broader plane, it was the failure of common law defences that led Americans to seek the sanction for their liberties in natural rights.[36] Both the context of the argument, and the language of the Declaration, show that to hold that individuals were endowed by their creator with rights that sprang equally from the very act of creation implied a commitment to create and maintain the basic human institutions that were needed to make those rights safe. As mere propositions, these claims were forms without content. The right to an institutional protection followed directly from the assertion of the abstract right. General principles, as has been suggested, could not determine the character of specific institutions; but on the other hand it would have to be admitted that the principles asserted would be politically meaningless unless supported by institutions. This necessity the Declaration recognized by stating that governments were instituted among men 'to secure these rights'. The position, however, did not appear at the time, to the men entrusted with legislative powers, to dictate any need for revolutionary changes in political structure, and the reasons for which Americans could, on the whole, accommodate their institutions to the demand for equal rights were quite logically consistent with their previous arguments. In the first place, as we have seen, the main body of their demand was for the equal protection of those common law rights which, as English subjects, were always theirs by birth—their birth-rights, as they said. But even when the entire body of their argument was lifted to the higher plane of natural rights, those rights did not seem to indicate the need for any more drastic change than could be brought about by reforming and adapting their existing institutions.

These views, unfortunately, did not complete a logically flawless circle for the independent Americans. For the Founders' conception of rights were not confined to equality; the idea of liberty, joined to that of property, played a more emotive and insistent part in their thoughts. Where liberty and equality ran any danger of being in competition with each other it was liberty that was sure to prevail, a matter of political experience, perhaps, even before it was one of principle. English history had already taught American Whigs that the chief danger to individual liberty came from over-mighty government. British imperial rule confirmed that lesson. It was to be amplified still further by the ensuing generation of American history, which had the important effect of teaching Americans that they needed to be as much on their guard against abuses from an excess of power at home as they had formerly against threats from overseas. Men who believed that governments had been instituted to secure their natural rights now confronted the bitter paradox that those rights were threatened by their own governments; this, for Jeffersonians, was the ominous lesson of the years of Federalist ascendancy. One result of the experiences out of which the American doctrine of individual rights was formulated was thus a kind of codification of something resembling an adversary relationship between the rights of the individual and the powers of government, and this codification took shape even while the Americans were in the process of building up an advanced form of representative government. That the rights of individuals were 'equal' was perhaps less important than that they were felt to need protection against government rather than by it; with the result that, beyond the formal constitutional safeguards, government in America in later generations was very slow to move to the defence of its individual citizens—and more especially when their very classification as citizens was in doubt, as with free Negroes. Certainly the American political system did little to encourage the view that government might be, or ought to be, the normal protector of equal rights through any continuous process of intervention or supervision.[37]

These were views upon which, in the pre-revolutionary years, American Whigs and Americans who were to become Tories, could find a good measure of common ground, and there was no ground on which they were more at home than that of the common law. Nor was this an ephemeral state of opinion. A century later, and after a great civil war, a justice of the Supreme Court could argue the case against monopolies with the assertion that the common law of England is the basis of the jurisprudence of the United States.[38] Their treatment at the hands of Parliament and the king convinced Americans that they were losing their common law rights; they were being held unequal under the law. It was in that context, and in the course of that argument, that they came to distinguish the problem of equality from the other issues of their time.

This is not to say that the idea of equality was to be limited to the common law concept. The great public proclamation of 1776 undoubtedly assisted in the gathering together of a variety of imperfectly formed but potent ideas that were already taking shape in people's minds. Effects were quickly felt in slave manumissions, in pungent expressions of social equality as a demand if not a fact, in the outcry against the 'unrepublican' features of the Society of the Cincinnati, and perhaps, in the long run, in the brevity of the period of effective Federalist rule. The majority principle in American politics owes its ideological edge to these ideas just as it owes its practical introduction to the political developments of the period. The concept of equality thus entered into the American political language, where it has sometimes been tortured but has never been dislodged.

NOTES

1. Benjamin H. Newcomb, *Franklin and Galloway: a Political Partnership*, New Haven and London, 1972, ch. 7.

2. *Diary and Autobiography of John Adams*, ed. L. H. Butterfield, Cambridge, Mass., 1961, II, 129–30

3. Daniel Dulany, *Considerations on the Propriety of Imposing Taxes in the British Colonies*, Annapolis, 1765, in Bernard Bailyn (ed.), *Pamphlets of the American Revolution*, Cambridge, Mass., 1965, I, 638.

James Otis, *The Rights of the British Colonies Asserted and Proved*, Boston, 1764, in Bailyn (ed.), *Pamphlets*, I, 452; and Bailyn's comment, I, 409.

4. Bailyn, ed., *Pamphlets*, I, 536.

5. Carl Becker, *The Declaration of Independence*, New York, 1922; repr. Vintage Books, 1942, p. 142.

6. John Dunn, *The Political Thought of John Locke*, Cambridge, England, 1969, pp. 222–8.

7. Ibid., p. 223.

8. Becker, op. cit., p. 147; Duncan J. MacLeod, *Racial Attitudes in Revolutionary and Early National America*, Cambridge Ph.D. thesis 1969; pp. 37–40, 43–4.

9. Thomas Jefferson, *A Summary View of the Rights of British America*, Philadelphia, 1774.

10. Richard Bland, *An Enquiry into the Rights of the British Colonies*, Williamsburg, 1769.

11. James Otis, *Rights of the British Colonies*, in Bailyn (ed.), *Pamphlets*, I, 438–9.

12. Otis, op. cit., 436–7.

13. For this development in general, see J. R. Pole, *Political Representation in England and the Origins of the American Republic*, London, 1966; Berkeley, 1971, pp. 170–2, 372–3, 248, 125–6, 317, 350, 535–6.

14. Otis, *Rights of the British Colonies*, 41 in Bailyn (ed.), *Pamphlets*, I, 449–450.

15. William Stubbs, *The Constitutional History of England*, Oxford, 1903, I, 505–12; 522.

F. W. Maitland, *Constitutional History of England*, Cambridge, 1919, pp. 22–3.

G. O. Sayles, *Medieval Foundations of England*, London, 1948, p. 343.

16. Nelson B. Lasson, *The History and Development of the Fourth Amendment*, Johns Hopkins University Studies, LV, no. 2, Baltimore, 1937, pp. 55–7.

17. L. H. Butterfield (ed.), *Diary and Autobiography of John Adams*, Cambridge, Mass., 1961, III, 211–12; *Diary of John Adams* in C. F. Adams (ed.), *Works*, Boston, 1850, II, 124.

18. Lasson, op. cit., pp. 59–63.

19. Lasson, op. cit., p. 43.

20. Rind's *Virginia Gazette*, 4 February 1768.

21. Purdie and Dixon's *Virginia Gazette*, 9 June 1774.

22. Dixon and Hunter's *Virginia Gazette*, 10 June 1775.

23. *State Trials*, ed. T. B. Howell, London, 1816, XIX, 1159ff.

24. Howell, *State Trials*, XIX, 1038–73.

25. Sir Charles Grant Robertson, *Select Statutes, Cases and Documents*, London, 1947, p. 455.

26. Colonial papers in which these events were relayed to American readers included *The Connecticut Courant*, *The New York Gazette*, *The New York Mercury*, *The Boston Gazette*, *The Massachusetts Gazette*, *The South Carolina Gazette*, and the several versions of the *Virginia Gazette*, to mention only a few.

John Wilkes and Isaac Barré had their names linked in a town in Pennsylvania, an association which drew disapproval from Namier, who felt that Barré's reputation deserved better treatment. L. B. Namier, *England in the Age of the American Revolution*, London, 1930, p. 263 n. 2. Otherwise, it is difficult to think of Britons, apart from the special case of Pitt, whom the Americans honoured in this way. Pittsburgh was so named by Forbes, but at least the name was retained. Francis Parkman, *Montcalm and Wolfe*, London, 1964, p. 464.

27. Lasson, op. cit., p. 65 n. 50.

28. O. M. Dickerson, 'Writs of Assistance as a Cause of the Revolution' in Richard B. Morris (ed.), *The Era of the American Revolution*, New York, 1939; repr. 1965, pp. 40–75.

Sir Charles Grant Robertson, op. cit., p. 454.

29. Dickerson, op. cit.

30. Purdie and Dixon's *Virginia Gazette*, 10 March 1768.

31. Hugh Blair Grigsby, *The History of the Virginia Federal Convention of 1788*, Richmond, 1890, I, 308.

32. J. R. Pole (ed.), *The Revolution in America, 1754–1788: Documents on the Internal Development of America in the Revolutionary Era*, London, 1970, pp. 482, 520 (Virginia, in which 'general warrants' are named), 531.

33. S. E. Morison (ed.), *Sources and Documents Illustrating the American Revolution, 1764–1788*, Oxford, 1962, p. 120.

34. Carl Ubbelohde, *The Vice-Admiralty Courts and the American Revolution*, Chapel Hill, 1960, pp. 15, 63, 64, 72–4, 90, 94; ch. 7; pp. 208–9.

Diary of John Adams, in *Works*, ed. C. F. Adams, 1850, II, 215–16.

35. Robert A. Rutland, *The Birth of the Bill of Rights, 1776–1791*, Chapel Hill, 1955, p. 36.

36. David S. Lovejoy, 'Rights Imply Equality: The Case Against Admiralty Jurisdiction in the American Colonies, 1764–76', *William and Mary Quarterly*, XVI, 4,

October 1959. Lovejoy speaks here of the Constitution, but the constitutional rights at issue could be traced to common law principles.

37. This procedure has become a normal attribute of government since the New York Fair Employment Practices Commission was established in 1945, followed by extensive and detailed legislation throughout the Northern States.

38. J. Field, dissenting in the *Slaughter House Cases*, 1873, 83 U.S. Wallace 16, p. 104.

In this work four historians explore the nature of American Loyalism and American Whiggism in 1776, and the significance of this first of modern civil and guerrilla struggles.

Esmond Wright in *The Loyalists in Britain* describes the experiences and the reactions of those Loyalists who came to and for the most part stayed in Britain; they found it, on the whole, a cold and unwelcoming place. Ralph Ketcham looks at Loyalty of another order in *Some Case Studies in Revolutionary Loyalty: Franklin, John Adams and Jefferson.* In *The Aftermath of Revolution: The Loyalists and British Policy* Charles Ritcheson traces the impact on British policy of the ending of the War of Independence, and in *Loyalists, Whigs and the Idea of Equality* J. R. Pole assesses the place of Loyalism and equality in the ideology of the Revolution.

Professor Esmond Wright is Director of the Institute of United States Studies in the University of London, Professor Ketcham is Professor of History at Syracuse University, Charles Ritcheson holds the Lovell Chair of History at the University of Southern California, and Dr J. R. Pole is Reader in American History and Government at the University of Cambridge and a Fellow of Churchill College.

£1.50 *net*   0 485 12902 7